DIVORCE
THE PAIN GOD
IS
ABLE TO HEAL

DIVORCE
THE PAIN GOD IS ABLE TO HEAL

Advantage
BOOKS

The way to breathe in freedom

ROBIN (ROCHEL) ARNE

Published by: ADVANTAGE BOOKS™, Longwood, FL, www.advbookstore.com

Unless otherwise indicated, Scriptures marked NIV are taken from the NEW INTERNATIONAL VERSION (NIV): Scripture taken from THE HOLY BIBLE, NEW INTERNATIONAL VERSION ®. Copyright© 1973, 1978, 1984, 2011 by Biblica, Inc.TM. Used by permission of Zondervan

Library of Congress Catalog Number: 2023935838

First Printing: April 2023
23 24 25 26 27 28   10 9 8 7 6 5 4 3 2 1

Acknowledgements

Christian fellowship brings a bounty of faith to my doorway. I walk with people of many talents who aid my construction of book material. I am thankful to all of them for their support. I lean on their wise counsel, and I learn by their hands. God has given me the ability to formulate thoughts that support Him and His profound way of being. I am blessed to serve Him in this manner. He never fails me, nor will He ever forget I pursue Him in love.

By His power, I am fed life and knowledge. I look to Him for all I am.

Table of Contents

Introduction

This book is for the person in need of love and care or support to the heart. If you suffer from a loss in marriage, God is the restorer of faith and hope. Through his person, we gain knowledge and find a way forward. God alone is the one to mend a tear-streaked heart. He grows the mind and reveals the love He holds for personal knowledge and hope. He orchestrates the desire to heal and mend by caring beyond the norm. Man inflicts loss, but with the Savior, a new thought process ensues where love abounds. A look at what God offers can bring to light the best factors of growth and unity. By harvesting the good God offers, one is never lost or in need because He is always making way for healing. He will shadow your thoughts and bring them home to Him personally, where you will learn and develop truth which in turn will light the path of unity. This is where the heart desires to rest and be restored. Dine with truth in this knowledge offering and be refreshed with honest intent, and a bounty of love will spring forth. You will have the knowledge necessary to act with confidence, and there will be an avenue for you to walk toward. Your intent will be of good, moral understanding, which in turn will bring you closer to Christ's way of thinking, where you will gravitate to the goal of freedom within your person. God is the caretaker and the way of love. Know Him personally and gain a reprieve. You will have support with a clear unity that binds the mind to the soft underbelly of a heart being restored. God is the Waymaker in whom all mankind can find peace and be at ease. God loves you. He is honest and genuine. He does not harm, nor will He embark on a mission of ill repute. He will guard your person, and you will learn a manner of gifted harmony where you will gain trust once more.

Robin (Rochel) Arne

Messages

1. The learning of mankind is from the hand of God. He supports mankind and gifts him with a miracle of truth when Jesus becomes the focal point of all thought processes.

2. God, the Father, is total and complete in His makeup. He holds mankind as His own. His love is always flowing, and He is rich in forgiveness.

3. God will teach mankind how to love and grow in faith. He is the Waymaker.

4. God will bring to light when a heart is in need of salvation. He speaks in a clear and thought-provoking manner.

5. God is righteous and true. He is bound by love and cannot sin. He is ever true.

6. God can perform as a Master in all He does.

7. God will lead with clear faith and restore the mind in care and support.

Robin (Rochel) Arne

Message One

The Learning of Mankind is From the Hand of God

He supports mankind and gifts him with a miracle of truth when Jesus becomes the focal point of all thought processes.

The power of the Savior is always the way to be secure. With God, man can build and find happiness and joy. God will enhance the mind and bring to light the process for opportunity, and reasonable care will ensue. When the table of truth is set, all of mankind gains in the manner of true commitment and honor. If someone fails in a task, God can lift the heart and build it anew. Look at how God operates. He paves the way for man to know Him by His Son, Jesus. Man does not find faith without pursuing the way of God. He must apply his heart and lean into the manner of true commitment. When this transpires, real change happens. With the goal of unity, there is no greater being to join with than the Savior Himself. All of God is beautiful. Through this knowledge, the heart discovers the mind can heal and thrive. God alone is the one who makes a seal with a graft to His person.

Should a person think to try to stand without the King as his leader, he will fail in some form or another. Healing of the heart ensues when the Lord is the salve and ointment. You will find this gem of knowledge is secure by reading the Book of enlightenment called the written Word of God. The Bible is a work that breeds true knowledge for man to learn. Each detail it presents is righteous and good. One never loses footing when truth is heard and received with honest faith. When God operates as a caregiver, one learns the way ahead in the fashion of good moral standing. God, the caretaker, organizes the mind and lifts the light of understanding toward the goal of bonding with a personal relationship toward His person. God leads and arrives at a goal with a true commitment, so none lose hope. If you invest in the Lord, you will find a way through the heartache of any loss. Divorce is a pain for both parties. Whether it be the one doing the paperwork and forcing the issue or the one regretting their partner's choice, both will feel like a failure in one form or another. God is the one who leads the pathway and opens the floodgate. With God, a person can find a way ahead and pursue the path of total unity with the King. This is how healing starts. All of mankind desires the knowledge God holds. God will deliver a heart to the knowledge there is a way forward. He will enlighten the mind and grace it with purity. The pain will dissolve, and a true commitment will ensue, but this only transpires when one applies the truth of God's Word to their way of thinking. God will shelter your mind and offer a pattern of growth where you can relate to His unity and find a goal of importance. Your value will be understood, and you will realize man falls short in many forms. This is why divorce takes place.

Man operates in a world of temptation where riches of the flesh are all around. The only way to stay connected to a unity of righteous care is to pursue the one who made you. He knows all your desires and can build upon them in a righteous manner, with no sin entering the pathway.

God knows how to mold your inner being, and He can bring to light what you desire is either false and not of Him, or it is light and brought by His hand. God does not orchestrate a broken goal of a former bond. He does not bring into play an outside influence of a negative action that leads to sin. God is righteous, and He cares for man in such a manner that all He does is good and uplifting.

If people follow the Lord, they will understand how to walk in the way of good, moral influence. God acts as the lead for all of mankind. He directs the union with a stand of integrity. Walking by way of the Master's hand offers one the gift of union where love and hope visit the mind and grace the heart with truth. By following the will of God, a person can gain intellect and be supported in a way that no other can offer. Leading the heart is a direct gift God can perform if you give Him the opportunity. God is the one all of mankind needs. Even the person who claims to have it all together needs the love of God in his life. God has stationed the heart to invest in His person, thus being tied to Him in a manner of life-giving wisdom and harmony.

When one is connected to the will of the Lord, he is invested in truth. God connects the heart and mind, and in doing so, He establishes the goal of a unified way of being. If a person desires to be at the helm of understanding, he needs to apply this principle to his way of operating. The goal of beauty will be achieved when one believes God is real and that He supports mankind. Telling the heart to subject itself to the will of God portrays a mindset of understanding in which one delves into the Word of truth and learns who has written and composed the knowledge it contains. God is the Waymaker who transcribes the mind to gather hope and gift it with the opportunity God puts forth. When you follow the way of the King, your heart will expand, and there will be healing. For every pain inflicted by another, there is significant growth if God's way of thinking is present. When the gift of faith is on the shelf, little improvement will be witnessed, but when faith is given flight, a whole bounty of opportunity begins to appear.

God can deliver man to a place of contented release when He is the one who is focused upon. Because man is geared to follow the lead of God, he mends when God becomes the timetable he follows and pursues. God leads with strength and gifts one with the same quality when prayer enters the stage of God's presence. When a person lifts up his Spirit in the direction of God, he grows in knowledge, and there is strength added unto him in such a way that he bends the pain, and it becomes minimal in its power to abscess his heart. The levitation of his joy unfolds, and soon a repair has transformed the mind, including a growth of will that accompanies the heart to God's favor. The light of God's hand forms a union so growth of good form can abound and bring the love of God to others in the pathway of the broken entanglement that once existed. Shouldering the heart alone only enhances the loss and makes the pain establish a deep crevasse in which doubt and anger breed.

Look to God for the complete truth of who you are as His child. This is where you will grow and invest in the truth of God's love for you. No one other than the Lord can harness pain and make it disappear from the thought process of loss. God offers a way to sustain in a time of heartache.

Through Him, one is gifted the amazing unity that brings a cure for the ailment that caused the misfortunate strike against a person's being. Through the care, the Lord manages the strike and makes it a mere scratch against the heart. You will remember the injury but no longer use it against yourself to inflict harm. When a person holds fast to the injury, he bleeds with raw anguish. It manifests and turns upon the individual, causing them to fall into depression with the thought there is no hope. God operates in a different unity branch. He showers the mind with the reality that He is a provider and a caretaker. Knowing that God's love is genuine makes you understand He does not cave or ever walk away. He stays perched at your side and graces your heart and mind with love.

Through Him, a blossoming effect can take shape. Bounty can be seen, and truth will abound in you where you will realize you haven't lost the most important gift a man can have—that which is ever faithful and secure. God is the only being who can stand through all difficulties and relationship goals. He is the Waymaker. He crafts the mind and feeds the soul with love and support to lift up and grant a desire for life where one is ever before God's throne. In the process, one gains the knowledge that with God, he is secure and steadfast through every process of every day.

God, the King Jesus, is the gift to mankind that abolishes pain and delivers it to His arm of strength to keep it at bay forever. If one thinks he alone can manage an onslaught of heartache, he is deceived. Walking in pain brings more deception and results in even more lies to the mind. You will build upon the loss and incorporate it into all you do. You may not understand your bitter outlook will affect others, but they will see your resentment, and it will harvest deceptive bounty just the same. God's power eliminates the desire and the manifestation of dark desires, and it brings to light the truth of how to pursue a goal of beauty. A healed mind can bring into play a viewpoint that God is the caretaker, and He has brought the gift of healing to the person who once only pursued revenge. God is the one to deliver a path of correction, not man. If you follow the lead God offers, your insight will ripen, and you will have custody of the pain and cause it to diminish. With God at the helm of your thinking process, you will have knowledge about how to obtain strength when dark thoughts intrude upon your mind. God delivers faith and support. He does not offer vengeful ideas or instructions on dark avenues to pursue.

If a capital of truth is what you seek, apply your will in the direct path of the King. He alone is the one to bring to light how to step and where to land with each undertaking you pursue. God cares more than any person has the ability to love, so you are granting favor to the Most High, and this shows wisdom. God the Father always invests His heart on the platter of good returns. He sees you as His own personal child, so understand He won't harm you in any form. By His power, you will engage in faith and be restored.

The Lord is the gift of love all of mankind desires to receive. God plants knowledge and brings the path of opportunity to the forefront, where the heart finds a place of beauty it can adhere to. God makes a life of care if you invest in His good way of faith. With the knowledge God grants, your heart will blossom and spread true gain to others and to your own personal ability to love and produce goodwill. The option to follow and pursue the God of all mankind is never without a good moral compass. God leads man, and he learns how to operate in the field of true gain. The leading God supplies is an investment that harbors the heart and feeds it good morsels of genuine influence where a person never faces the trial of doubt without the true understanding God is always present to learn by.

If you pursue the faith, the Lord presents, you will learn a way of being that supports the good manifested in the Word of God. This understanding underlines a better way of life. You will acknowledge the truth and build upon its stand. When this transpires, your heart gains nutrients that upload a moral bounty of fruit found only in the scriptures. Always look to the Word of the Lord to gain insight and understanding of good therapeutic knowledge. God is the one who created the Book of truth. He offered it as a gift to learn about Him. Because the Word of God is crafted by Spirit and truth, it is infallible. When God is at the helm of your workmanship, you will see true unity in which your heart and His are connected. God fosters the care and brings into play a path in which the mind is grafted to knowledge and support. God is the Waymaker. He never builds without a plan or way of completion. Teach this truth to yourself as a way of gaining strength. You will open the door to a better self-image that supports the truth you are tied to the real King, Jesus. He is man's greatest gift from above, God the Father. Salvation is the way to a life of a forgiven venue. God brought forth this measure so all of mankind could be set free. One needs only to believe and profess faith and have acceptance of Jesus' death upon the cross. It is what seals the deal and makes it bound as one.

Gaining faith-based love produces a concrete material that enables the heart to build and sustain any hardship. God's power is absorbed and fed into the mind alongside the Spirit, and beauty is created. All God presents is solid and administers love and support through harmony with Him personally. If one tries to enter into a stance where God is not supported, he will learn that the bounty is not forthright. The gain will reflect a dark impression, and there will only be a heavy foundation of negative crafting. Many find hope is false when they try to manipulate a way of action or gain. It leads to loss in the outcome, so realize it is wise to formulate an authorship plan based on truth and genuine care of support. God can build a foundation where a new plan unfolds where a dark adventure was the goal. God can brighten an outlook with a direct cure of light if a person decides the path to beauty is found in God's person rather than self-alignment.

A plan of support is by far the proper way to act in comparison to reaching for a mistake and hoping it will lead to growth. God builds with love and harmony. He never builds with a negative bounty as a source of gain. If you feel attached to a dark desire, you are not in His will. He will not bring a return that does not glorify His person, and you will only acquire a misnomer of guilt and doubt. A question mark will always lie in your path, and you won't be blessed by the Father's hand. God can restore a landmark and make it right. He can craft a plan where all your goals align with Him personally. Finding the way ahead will arrive when the timing is set and God releases the open doorway to your understanding. At times the wait can be tedious but know God operates not as man operates but with the perfect ability to bring about the best outcome for all parties involved.

With the knowledge God builds in a formula only He can comprehend, lean into the strength it offers by supporting His care to your Spirit. Let God manifest your goal set and be contented knowing a good return is on the horizon. God organizes the mind and resides in the Spirit as the Holy Ghost. The Father speaks through the Spirit, and you learn His will and know His leadership when you apply the truth of God's Word to the situation. God leads you with a whisper and a gentle nudge, producing a sound understudy of leadership where you gain insight and guidance with clear hope and solid understanding as a goal.

Look to Christ for a path of hope. He develops the heart and makes it a bounty holder where your love is made manifest. The Lord is by far superior to all of mankind. God is at work supporting the mind. In Him, man has a structure to pursue and can operate in good care. God, the Father, is ever faithful. God is a source of hope. He establishes the heart to love and connect with His person. In Christ, one gains the insight into knowing a righteous walk and how to proceed in a daily walk of light. If instruction is your gain, you will glean knowledge when you administer to the mindset God is a leader of good, righteous endeavors. Through His person, you will understand a way forward, and the light of love will be ever before your thought process. Look to scripture to better realize whom to pursue. You will find faith and the support your heart desires on the throne of integrity with a backdrop of saving grace as your guidance counselor.

If a person needs hope, the will of the Father will lead him on the path of right thinking. This happens while man invests in the true pursual of King Jesus. God is ever with the man who invites His presence into his person. The law of man states no one is above his own understanding, but this is not the case if unity with God is adhered to. God makes a way for man to know Him personally and for growth to be a way forward in trust. With Jesus, a plan of beauty will unfold, and knowledge will come forth. God continuously invests in His people. How they apply the gift of His person is dependent on whether they truly accept Jesus as Lord and caretaker of their lives.

God lifts up man to know the true value of a heart by way of a witness known as the salvation message. It holds fast to the true nature of God in that the Father gave His only Son to be a statement of great value. There is no greater value than accepting Jesus as your personal Savior. God is the caretaker of all mankind. He is the reason man exists. By His person, man can gain entry to heaven itself. God holds man as His own personal child. Each person is a creation of the Most High. Each has value, and everyone is supported by the hand of God. God instructs the heart, and He develops the mind to support the good of mankind. All people need one another to develop a solid unity where love flows.

God always operates in the realm of truth. He is always an influence of true, moral guidance that is always pure. God the Father supports man in the way of a leader who has a solid identity of good, moral conduct. Christ is the foundation of faith where man can be united as a body of one. Learning by applying the truth of God's Word to the goal of bonding with Him is solid in its design. God has placed His Word in the form of the Bible so man can gain insight into His character and grow in wisdom. Look to scripture for understanding and knowledge to better grasp the unity God offers.

The Lord Almighty is with us; the God of Jacob is our fortress. Psalm 46:7 NIV

God desires for man to know Him like a father knows his child. We do this by embracing God as a caregiver and a supporter of man. Truth unfolds when one applies the knowledge God offers through His Bible, and spiritual harmony develops. God will guide a mind into the light where truth will be recognized and accepted. When this application takes root, a heart learns who to follow. With God, favorable decisions begin to form, and enlightenment ensues.

Man invests in a management style that is apart from the King. He does not comprehend that he needs a Savior who can organize his heart and give his person the strength of what to perceive. God is order, and He reflects a path of support that unifies man to Himself. The King Jesus is wholesome and pure. All He offers is perfect and of sound principles. When one searches for truth, he gains the upper hand in that his life will be based on unity with the caregiver, and growth will occur that reflects good moral conduct.

The light of the Savior is for man to better himself. The Lord Jesus is a true minister of love and hope. His value far surpasses that of any one person or thing. God has a balance where His heart is justified beyond that of man. God can heal and support any wound inflicted on your person. Pain is not reflective of God's love. It happens to all of mankind at some point in their life. How one handles grief and injury is based on the belief of whether one can wash it away or whether God can do the restoration. The latter brings true healing salve that lasts a lifetime. God's power unfolds through the work of prayer and the belief that He is all-powerful. This truth is known, and a bounty of rewards can be harvested. God creates the mind and heart to act in accordance with His way of being. When we apply this principle, we learn hope is at the door, and we can step through the doorway and gain freedom. With God the Father, our desires are made manifest if they align with His way of being. We can glean a true support beam in the manner of grafted witness material where all we think and apply are made whole because He is the Waymaker. Our talent is by His hand alone, so know you have a way ahead if you harness your heart to the Lord Himself.

God is always faithful. The Lord is not harmful or supportive of a dark idea in any form. When God is at work, there is beauty and truth. The favor of God comes when the heart believes upon His person and supports the Lord Jesus Christ as the Waymaker. The triumph of Jesus is written on every page of the Word of God. You can find truth in all the messages offered. Nothing is dark or dense in the way of negative understanding. Each Bible story holds character, and it portrays how man should operate and where he can build in character according to the Lord's design and flavor of life. The trial expressed in the page of atonement is not grafted, so man would embark on death to clear his name. This is not possible without the blood of Jesus. Jesus is the only way to have eternal life. We do not understand the power of His blood completely, but we know it is real, and it supports the body of faith we call the bride. Anyone in need of a fresh unity in the way of love and guidance can build in the manner of great care by leaning into the one called Savior. This is Jesus. He is eternal and freely gives the gift of His sacrifice to mankind. All of man can know Him personally by pressing ahead and showing support in His direction. A small dose of faith can move a mountain. This is discussed in the Book of John. Look at the verses below and learn the truth.

"For God so loved the world that he gave his one and only Son, that whoever believes in him shall not perish but have eternal life. 17 For God did not send his Son into the world to condemn the world, but to save the world through him. John 3:16-17 NIV

Message Two

God the Father is Total and Complete in His makeup

He holds mankind as His own. His love is always flowing, and He is rich in forgiveness.

The beauty of the King is He supports all of mankind. He offers each person a way to know Him as their personal Savior. He is rich with opportunity and care. By His person, none shall perish if they have chosen Him to be their offering of love. If a person believes in faith that God is who He claims to be a bond is created, and a length of rope is adhered from one heart to another. It unites the pair, and they, in turn, act as one. No hardship is greater than the power of God to heal the damage or misfortunate injury. God alone is the one to bring to light a path of opportunity where love and support both reside. By the grace of the King, many have found the life of true commitment to be supportive in nature. A believer who has extended their union through study and application to the Word God offers freely will know the personal connection that leads and directs in good form. God offers all of mankind this bond and free extension of Himself. It is up to the individual to apply and take it upon His own platter, the gift of power that completes the connection and brings the bounty of true bonded crafting to life. A letter of reference is not what brings one to the throne of God. It is the desire to know Him personally and to build the unity portrayed at the cross of redeeming power. The offering was given so man may know the Lord as His personal guidance counselor. In doing so one gains the insight and the spiritual connection to further advance in the manner of justice personified.

God releases a hold in the form of glue that sets the spirit in the palm of his hand, never to fall away or lose its place within the family of God's own being. God, the caretaker, is always a Waymaker. Through His unity, man is informed how to proceed in life so as not to fall into the depth of darkness where loss is all that is known. God protects the heart and fastens the mind to build faith that resonates with hope and structure. Because God leads, we can know harmony and a way forward. We can dine on the build of good form and be safe in the harbor of a guided minister of integrity. We alone cannot perform much in the way of the substantial bounty that brings light to mankind or our own platform. We can't climb the heights of good form, nor do we limit our control in the manner of dark response. Only God can define us as pleasing in the spirit, but this won't happen without the firm hand of the Lord embellishing our hearts with true character and subsequent knowledge of who He is and what He operates as.

The Father of all mankind is supportive and great in the mind of the one who pursues knowledge and truth. God the Father never rejects a person, nor will He make them fall away. If you have stepped outside of His good will, know He will gather you to Himself if you offer your heart toward His person. Believing in the Savior is a must. He is the Master of all. With Jesus at the helm of your life, you will find a way that is presentable and forthright. Man can lose footing, but God alone is the one to align the heart and mind for His good.

Look to the need of another, and you will understand the way God operates. He is steadfast in His authorship of unity, and from His hand, one learns the truth. God is personal. He offers His unity on a platter of divine giftedness where you will learn who you are with Him as your guide and counselor. God holds all of mankind in the palm of His hand. He never leads in the dark or without purpose. God relates to man in a personal manner. The heart of man hears God speak even if it doesn't recognize it is Him presenting the undertaking of good form. God has balance and unity when He builds. Through His direct way of being we find love and care with a measure of good hope and beauty. All God creates is glorifying to Him personally. We may not always realize how our offerings are intertwined with His goal sets, but we can trust our work brings a good form in one gift or another. If you offer your talent without the restraint of payment needed, you are gifting others with a bounty that reflects God's good character. Yes, man needs to make a living, but it is with the heart that God measures wealth. If your talent is a rare study that gifts a person with a way ahead and you deliver that offering in the form of the passage of care, you are supporting the Lord and His way. All of mankind has some form of gift to better teach and support others in their daily walk. You may not be a surgeon, but even a bricklayer has talent. Each gift is needed. One is for the betterment of health and the other is for comfort in the way of shelter against the elements of weather. Unity is the basis for both of these. God operates in the manner of talent to gain His people a way ahead, whether in the form of a gift of love or a trinket of strength that incorporates the heart with the knowledge one is thought of on a personal level.

The God of mankind is supportive in His way of good care. He binds the loss one feels and gifts it with a new outlook where hope prevails and sin is erased. Pain is often brought upon a person by the injury of another who strikes against his person. Forgetting the knowledge of the King brings a path of destruction into the scene. Only by incorporating the love of God is one able to invest in growth that leads to healing. The heart connects with an injury, but it doesn't know how to repair the pain without reading the Word presented in the Bible. The knowledge of God's Word grafts to the mind a way forward where pain is set aside, and personal gain becomes the landmark of the mind. Pain festers when salve is not applied to the root of the problem. God's Word acts as a catalyst where unity is fed, and growth in love encloses the scar tissue. Pain will adhere to the heart and cause more doubt or sin nature if not controlled by the truth of God's Word. Only then does one invest in the truth of love provided from God's hand.

God brings to the table a better way forward in that He knows the wound and how to recover its depth. Pain is bred only when one pursues it as a home base. The application of love brings to the table a way of healing that brings to light a vested understudy that teaches the heart and mind the way of God and His attributes. God's voice releases the mind where the fruit of the vine can begin to bloom. When this develops, the heart engages, and the unity from God to the person is felt and received as grace, where hope begins to be harvested. With a future on the horizon that speaks of light and unity, a person desires more of the freedom God brings into play.

The truth presented by unity in the form of trust and hope is derived by investing in the one of great magnitude. He is the great I Am. No one ever loses when God is his focus. With the Lord, all of mankind has the opportunity to be light to others and gain in the way of invested grace, which in turn brings healing and hope. God's power is justified and supports the knowledge that no other is greater than God Himself. With this manifested understanding, a mind gravitates to the great I Am, and false descriptions of authorship leave, and in its place are love and purity. God the Father cares deeply for all of mankind. There is not one person He steps away from. He is always at work restoring and leaning into His people. He makes a way for growth and supports healing with care and knowledge that surfaces in the form of love and heart-felt beauty described in the Book of Judges. Read below and learn the truth about who the Lord is and how He operates.

> *When the angel of the Lord appeared to Gideon, he said, "The Lord is with you, mighty warrior." 13 "But sir," Gideon replied, "if the Lord is with us, why has all this happened to us? Where are all his wonders that our fathers told us about when they said, 'Did not the Lord bring us up out of Egypt?' But now the Lord has abandoned us and put us into the hand of Midian." 14 The Lord turned to him and said, "Go in the strength you have and save Israel out of Midian's hand. Am I not sending you?" "But Lord, "Gideon asked, "how can I save Israel? My clan is the weakest in Manasseh, and I am the least in my family" 16 The Lord answered, "I will be with you, and you will strike down all the Midianites together." Judges 6:12-16 NIV*

God brings the knowledge of good strength to man, meaning He supports the heart when it is tied to His person and bending toward the good, He offers. All the unity in the Father and His person is binding, and longevity is at hand. God, the Father, is always faithful. Through His personage, man can find faith and be lifted to the height of ever after in an eternal unity that supports him for a lifetime. God is the one who cares and crafts the goal of support only He can provide. God offers man the hope of salvation and through this gateway man is able to ascend to the throne of the King called the great I Am.

The leadership from the Lord is ever right and sacred. You will find faith at the core of the bounty He brings to the table. God is all-powerful, and through His person, one gains entry to the promised land of heaven. Look at how God has brought the people of years past through the desert and offered peace and unity through the trial of conquered land.

> *When you go to war against your enemies and see horses, chariots, and an army greater than yours, do not be afraid of them because the Lord your God, who brought you up out of Egypt, will be with you. 2When you are about to go into battle, the priest shall come forward and address the army. 3He shall say: "Hear, O Israel, today you are going into battle against your enemies. Do not be fainthearted or afraid; do not be terrified or give way to panic before them. 4 For the Lord your God is the one who goes with you to fight for you against your enemies to give you victory." Deuteronomy 20:1-4 NIV*

The Lord is a Savior who organizes the heart and offers it truth in the way it should operate. God gifts man with knowledge and the unity that brings to life the gain of His person. Our Lord is stable in all He upholds. You can count on His administering way to be just. The love of the Father is always present, and Jesus, His Son, is masterful as well. The two act as one where they both are tied together by the heart with the same goal set. God favors man when he decides to offer his way of life to the knowledge that God is the all in all. Each opportunity offered from the hand of the Mighty one is a gift that supports the knowledge God is real, and the great I Am is understood. Gain is had by applying your goal to that of God. Good growth occurs when you place Him at the helm of your life. A way forward ensues, and a door of life will be appropriated. God is a miracle worker. He offers life ever after, and the gain of this action produces a heart of beauty and nourished mannerisms. God is the one who builds with character. Only in Him is there light, so one must lean into God to know His person. It is with knowledge that truth and enlightenment are bound. God is the Waymaker. His person supports the logic that man is not above the heart of God. God is a union of love for man. When you trust the Lord, you gain growth, and hope comes onto the scene. If pain is at your door, remember the Savior gifted you with a love so rich none can compare. God's love is stable and never fleeting. His love binds the heart and mind, and care ensues and overflows with goodness. God is far superior to man in the way He supplies the body of faith with stable support at all times. Pain ensues when man drifts from the truth God has portrayed in His Word, the Bible. Following the voice of God offers real unity.

Trust the leadership of the Savior and know you are safe in His presence. The light from God's hand can support your heart and offer a pure understanding of the light you need to heal or be supported by. With God, all things align, and true commitment is adhered to. God offers the heart a unity that supports knowledge and gifts the mind with the revelation unity is all important. God is the one to bind your spirit with. In Him is found a union where strength and knowledge intertwine. No one has ever lost when it comes to the favor of the Lord. He releases the bondage and grafts to the heart, a clear viewpoint that brings to light that man is fallible. God, the creator, lifts the heart and brings it to a place of clear advancement. He showers the mind with individual grafting, where a union of beauty takes form. Without His aid, the mind engages in dark processes, always trying to gain freedom, but no relief comes. Only when the Savior is called upon does a soul develop true caresses of love where truth presents the plan of bounty to aid in the process of healing. Allow the Savior the freedom to work through the pain, and you will have an insight that bleeds justice, and righteousness will unfold. How this takes form is only by the hand of God. One is not able to make the process happen. Only the union with God will bring this change. Trust His timing and the growth will be felt.

God is the King man desires to know. This is why a person leans into the care God offers him. Alone, man tries to gain a way of purity, but he does not hold the redemptive manner nor does he have saving power. God delights when man applies his mind to His goal of union. The timing of healing depends on the way one invests and operates toward the person of Jesus. God waits patiently, and He invests according to His design. God will work miracles if you believe His good nature is for your betterment. Think about the way Jesus died on the cross and how His blood was pure as it ran down His forehead. All the while transforming the world and its representation of negative attributes called sin. God brought to man the release needed to gain a way of redemption. Through the blood the Lord shed, a new path was formed, and gain was administered. God's bond is royal and blue meaning His way is righteous and just. Just as the flag of remembrance for our nation signifies freedom and harmony for man the cross distinguishes Jesus as Lord. You can find truth concerning what took place in the words below.

> *In the same way, the chief priests, the teachers of the law, and the elders mocked him. 42 "He saved others," they said, "but he can't save himself! He's the King of Israel! Let him come down now from the cross, and we will believe in him. 43 He trusts in God. Let God rescue him now if he wants him, for he said, "I am the Son of God.'" 44 In the same way, the robbers who were crucified with him also heaped insults on him. 45 From the sixth hour until the ninth hour darkness came over all the land. 46 About the ninth hour Jesus cried out in a loud voice, "Eloi, Eloi, lama sabachthani?" -which means, "My God, my God, why have you forsaken me?" 47 When some of those standing there heard this, they said, "He's calling Elijah." Immediately one of them ran and got a sponge. He filled it with wine vinegar, put it on a stick, and offered it to Jesus to drink. 49 The rest said, "Now leave him alone. Let's see if Elijah comes to save him." And when Jesus had cried out again in a loud voice, he gave up his spirit. Matthew 27:41-50 NIV*

The Father of Jesus knew what needed to transpire for mankind to know His person. Without the blood of Jesus, no person would gain entry to the great I Am. The host of heaven is ever faithful. The recognition of God's power is what claimed the saved from certain death. Only His abundant measure of grace is what secures our home in the kindest of formations. Only God can perform in such a manner and still live and breathe. Man gained a measure of love no other can compare to. Jesus had a willing spirit, and He paved the doorway for all mankind to know Him as Lord. We have the opportunity to better equip our hearts in such a way that we gain knowledge and a gift of unity when we call on Jesus for salvation. He is ever faithful to support our request if our hearts are yielded in care. Look to Christ for the knowledge and care that binds and grafts with grace. The Lord is by far superior to that of man. Through Jesus, we know how to gain freedom through unity that enhances the heart and lifts the spirit. God delivers our mind to the goal of union so we are better equipped to move with ease. Our mind gains understanding, and we operate with care in the way we present as a whole. Never doubt the bond of the Lord to your person. He will always engage with you and offer a plan of pure motive that harbors the heart in a shoreline of integrity.

Look at how God presented His Son to the world. He did it in the manner of hidden intent thus making a pathway for the salvation experience to unfold. Had Satan known the true purpose of Jesus, he would have sought to destroy him before He was born. Jesus was protected by the Father, and He never suffered without a willing purpose for mankind. God the Father was not harsh; He was a Waymaker in whom the Lord Jesus trusted and believed. We, the people of the bride of God, understand the meaning of true repentance, and a reflective way of thinking is our goal. We do not stand to serve ourselves. Our purpose is for others to gain the knowledge we hold within our person. The gift of unity God provides is always righteous and clear. God leads and connects with our being, and we gain perspective with good insight and clear mental importance. Without the gift of God to His people, man would not know peace. The center of God's heart is built with us in mind. We are the ones He loves to pursue. He does not step outside the parameter of true Lordship; however, He lifts our hearts and minds in His direction. When we unite with God, our insight begins to blossom and we find a unity of pure power known as salvation, where we are tied to the Savior for all time. This experience plays a role in how we invest our hearts and minds. Look at the way God presented Jesus to man. The below verses recite the care of a God who uses people of all standings. Rich or poor does not matter to the King named God.

So Joseph also went up from Nazareth in Galilee to Judea, to Bethlehem, the town of David, because he belonged to the house and line of David. 5 He went there to register with Mary, who was pledged to be married to him and was expecting a child. 6 While they were there, the time came for the baby to be born, and she gave birth to her firstborn, a son. She wrapped him in cloths and placed him in a manger because there was no room for them in the inn. Luke 2:4-6 NIV

The Lord was born a pauper with no income or vast wealth that man could understand. But in reality, He owned the whole world. All of creation was at His fingertips as he was the creator and the maker of all things. He sat at the right hand of the Father before time began. Only God understands the completeness of this, but His Word supplies us with the knowledge God the Father and Jesus are one. Included in this is the Holy Spirit. He counsels us daily, and we are guided by His voice. You may not recognize when God speaks, but He is faithful just the same. Guidance is a gain offered to mankind with no price tag attached. Only God is all-knowing. In Him is found strength and love that supports our being in true beauty and care. God leads, and we follow if our hearts are joined to His person. When you accept the gift of salvation, a guarantee of unity springs forth. By working with God, you will have unity and support in a way of true honor ship. God is our Waymaker in whom we can build and create without fear of being taken advantage of. God does not invest unwisely, so He can't be manipulated or pushed in the direction of ill-gotten gain. If you try to build and create on your own, a blend of doubt and insecurity will frame your heart. You may neglect the love of one to another and walk in the way of darkness. God restores vision when prayer is offered, and sincerity returns.

Leading others is not always calm waters. There may be discord and issues that arise where prayer and support from the Master's hand needs to be applied. The best-run operation believes and works as a team under the leadership of Christ the King. If you practice the principles described in the Book of love known as the Word of God, you will have the skill set to serve a team of builders. God cares about all of mankind. In Him is the reward of a balanced undertaking that guides with support and becomes a union in its design. There may be hiccups along the way, but light and understanding will unfold, and you will have clear vision.

Pain can be managed in the same manner. Apply the learned principles of team management and operate as though God is the reason for your desire for healing. The way a person views healing is what will determine the salve he applies to the wound that has been inflicted. The Savior is one who pulls the mind into the support beam of love. Through the character of God, man gains the knowledge that a superior being is at work. Christ the King is always within reach. You need only to pray and accept His good care. By His person, man can be reformed when an ache has been administered. Pain need not control your heart or your thought processes. With Jesus, one can learn how to operate with a new design and lean into the knowledge God brings to life where ground has been broken. Your heart is a gift where love is to reside. God made man to be content in the home of His crafting. God developed a manner of true intent when He prompted the heart to receive and be led by His hand. If you fall into the thought process that God has removed His hand from your person, you are mistaken. The only time God leaves a person's side is when He has been asked to do so, and even then, He stands at the ready to guide and support should the individual realign his intent and turn to the King for aid.

The skill of a man is to better aid instruction for many to learn from. With God, all talent is known and multiplied. The heart of man proves frail, but God is not that way. God always stays committed and never accepts defeat when it comes to unity. If you struggle believing God supports your person, remember who He offered as proof of His love to all mankind. He wasn't stingy in who he granted salvation. This should alleviate any doubt or misgivings you have concerning the character of God's care. Look to scripture to understand who the Savior of the world is. You can find many verses pertaining to the way He lived and supported man. Below is one example of this.

21Leaving that place, Jesus withdrew to the region of Tyre and Sidon. 22 A Canaanite woman from that vicinity came to him, crying out, "Lord, Son of David, have mercy on me! My daughter is suffering terribly from demon-possession." 23 Jesus did not

answer a word. So his disciples came to him and urged him, "Send her away, for she keeps crying out after us." 24 He answered, "I was sent only to the lost sheep of Israel." 25 The woman came and knelt before him. "Lord, help me! She said. 26 He replied, "It is not right to take the children's bread and toss it to their dogs." 27 "Yes, Lord," she said, "but even the dogs eat the crumbs that fall from their masters' table." 28 Then Jesus answered, "Woman, you have great faith! Your request is granted." And her daughter was healed from that very hour. Matthew 15:21-28 NIV

God does not require man to invest economically for Him to build a heart of purity. God looks to the spirit of a man not his pocketbook. How you endeavor to pursue the King determines whether you are anchored in His will or just working in hopes of a gain for yourself outside of the desire for a better unity with Jesus at the helm. The Lord supports a person when the goal of trust is what is put forth. The partnership requires faith and the commitment to true worship with the action of prayer and invested love. God will supply the love on His end. The remainder is up to you. If you ask God to give you faith, He will hear your words and deliver an abundance, so you will see a growth in your heart that speaks of a union where you desire more of God. You won't look at the Lord as a giver of fruit until you truly connect with His person. For this to happen, you need to spend time reading the Bible. It is His instruction manual, which builds in the way of contented unity pointed to God above. In hearing of the Word, you will gain an important unity that will lead to growth where your heart expands and leans into the Savior. In turn, this builds the bond, breaks the negative strands that encase a soul, and refreshes it with hope. Think on the way God has built truth for the nation of Israel through the generations. He has guided this people group and returned them to their homeland even though they were scattered across the globe prior to the call He placed upon their hearts. Through the process of strength, God delivered Israel safe and secure with a place to prosper and live in peace. God is faithful to all who serve Him in trust and unity.

The Lord cares for the ones who pursue His person even during difficult times. This is when He can carry the burden someone is under. God is always at work creating and building good conduct within the heart. Adversity brings a strong desire to lash out and strike against the manifest of difficulty but take the road of Christ. You will be better equipped to walk with care and know peace as a result. Guidance from God is support no man can achieve even in the greatest of times, for the Lord grants knowledge and insight alongside opportunity that lasts for all eternity. God is a factor where all of mankind can build and be safe as a result. However, mankind is not aware of the great I Am unless he applies his heart and thinking toward the unity God portrays. This happens because the Lord administers a direct support application in the form of grace and hope. He is the only supplier of these two gifts. It is by the hand of God that we have stability within our hearts. Take into account the way God aided man in the days of Noah. An ark was built by a man who trusted the King and believed the words He spoke. God offered a reprieve against the coming flood because Noah was found to be uncorrupted by sin. Yes, he did have sin, but not to the extent he was overcome with it, such as the rest of mankind was. Look to scripture and see how kind God was to Noah because he was faithful in his walk with the Most High.

So the Lord said, "I will wipe mankind, whom I have created, from the face of the earth-men and animals, and creatures that move along the ground, and birds of the air-for I am grieved that I have made them. " 8 But Noah found favor in the eyes of the Lord. Genesis 6:7-8 NIV

God supports man and all of his dreams when there is unity in the invested thought process. God honors things that support the well-being of all. He does not invest when there is darkness present. If you desire the will of the Father, you will find a true connection when you read His Bible truths. You will gain and accept the honor and namesake of Jesus. When you lean into the Savior, you understand the true meaning of good and just ventures. God builds where He is welcomed. He does not uplift in the manner of unjustified gain. That is not who He is as a manifested being. God is honor and right sentiments at all times. Through the love of the

Savior, one can gain the support and hope that is needed to regain a loss and be healed of a hurt that infests the spirit. Divorce is a scar when the salve of love has been anointed to the broken jar of division. A marriage is a union of the heart and mind. It was made to stand for a lifetime.

However, when a division transpires, the loss is crippling to many who have experienced this pain. Usually, there is always one individual who remains faithful, and they are the ones to inherit the damage sustained by the loss. When a person feels pain, he looks to himself for guidance, but this does not aid him. When a heart seeks to learn the way of God, it becomes soft and subtle, where love is grown. God brings to the heart a way to heal and accept the injury without feeling neglected or stricken with hate. The Savior brings light and encouragement when He is believed in. By trusting in the leadership of the Most High, a person will lose the intent of dark thoughts and step where the Lord guides. The ground will be solid and secure, and a healing transformation will ensue. Often people think staying inside the boundary of doubt and pain brings a strength that holds the heart at bay. In reality, all that transpires is a hatred where no gain can be had. Forgiveness feeds the mind and spirit with the goal of unity in the Father and His good moral way of being. A shoulder to cry on may bring a person toward another, but only God can bring a significant change in healing. All the intent of man never holds fast to the way of justice. It will seek revenge, and heartache will be the bounty. On the onset of an injury, let God be the way you choose to follow. This will prepare you for a fast recovery, and you will be pleasing to others who engage with your person. Bitterness is recognized and seen as an ugly personality trait. No one enjoys being around a dark manner where love has fallen away to be replaced by a gestation of unhappy thoughts and actions. People who have turned toward the light are more equipped to bring the knowledge of the saving power of God to others. They themselves have learned the key to real commitment and how to be a stable benefactor of the gift of love God brings to all when He is welcomed in. Leading others is a stronghold if Christ is the head of all you do. God will open wounds and pour salve into them to remove the sting, and only a gentle memory is left.

God brings unity and hope in ways no other can organize or lead in. If you desire a heart of beauty, fall in love with the King. His care is far superior to that of any man, and He supports you with total grace. God is not harsh, nor is He about redefining who you are as a person. He desires for you to know Him personally and to build in the manner of grace and hope. These are support measures that inflict the gift of union where you always reside in the care of a greater connection that, in turn, delivers healing and growth. This builds a character and measures it with progress leading to a clear developmental build in the heart and mind that speaks of invested opportunity. God enjoys leading us to the light. He supports our hearts and minds when we believe He is real. He works as a unity maker and through His person we are made whole in the way of integrity and forthright manners. Our walk in the way of the light builds us up into a good moral influence that invests in others with support and good aptitude abilities. God the Father always works for the good of our being. He never works against us in the way of harm. Discipline may come on the scene if sin is present but know God is not one to inflict a strike without purpose. When God corrects our sinful life, it is for the better of our walk with Him. It is much more prosperous to stay walking in the way of God than to step in the way of the negative. The negative brings a fall in one form or another. There is never gain when one pursues a dark endeavor. Know the King and form a union with His spirit. Knowing God and serving His will is better than gaining the world and losing your soul.

The management of life is in God's hands. He organizes the thought process and delivers a bounty that transforms the outreach of the heart. If ever you find a loss has transpired within your life, lean into the Savior and trust His perspective. His Bible is clear with truth and how to manage a heart. He leads with clear support, and He will offer you a lifeline where you gain aid, and a goal of beauty will unfold. The power of the King is made manifest within you when you apply Biblical teachings to your way of being. The God of the Bible never fails to outdo our understanding. He is far superior to us in all things, right and just. God teaches man how to value one another and live according to a standard that is rich and supports the life and purity of mankind. When Biblical standards are reached, a heart engages in trust and develops good intent. This is what makes a believer stand out when adversity comes his way. How one works toward the goal of union in the care of others balances where the mind wanders. The love of the King guides the mind on a path of resolute knowledge where a realization that God brings life to any devastation or injury heightens the manner of life-giving ideas and leads a person down the path of righteousness. Knowing how to operate in the realm of distinction offers a mindset where unity and progress of light flow as one. God is the Waymaker. He leads with truth and guidance that envisions a heart with clear mental gain.

The power of Jesus' name alone transforms and with it comes the gift of unity and light. Jesus transforms lives for the better. No person who has ever truly acknowledged the saving power of Christ ever steps back from the truth it presents. Christ the Savior is righteous and true. In His person, one finds favor that represents hope and love. God is always a forward way of being. In Him is the pathway to good form. God does not harvest a lie or put forth devastation, so if you have been injured, it is not from the hand of God. He does, however, bring into play a corrective measure if you pursue evil in place of good. God never harms the mind. He gives clear mental gain when He puts forth an idea or an understanding. It is not due to God's hand upon your heart if you are confused in your thought process. Satan often presents as a manifestation of enticement where another option can seem profound but in reality, he can only bring harm and loss. Marriage is a union of one man to one woman. If you are enticed to betray your marriage vows, it is not a gift from the Lord. You can bank on the truth that such a desire has come straight from the pit of hell. The desire to stray is a lure from the hand of the false God. It is evil, and it will bring deception that carries to the heart of a man. Many have fallen prey to the lie God brings new beginnings by way of a new partner more suited to a new way of life or thinking. This is not the way of the Lord. The union of marriage is sacred to God. He does not unbind what He brought together. If you are struggling with which way to pursue your goal for the future, remember God creates a union in the palm of His hand. No danger can manifest unless a person grants the deception a home front. Leading the mind to the format of sexual pleasure will end in despair. Sex is pure when it is contained within the marriage bed. Outside of this is evil cloaked in carnal releases. God does not desire man to operate on bodily appetites. With Him, there is substance and truth.

The more one delves into the dark entanglements, the more deceived he becomes. Look at where man has fallen from. Days from the past life of those that were in the Bible share the honor of man to God. You can find proof of this in the Bible. Look to Abraham and how he stayed committed to his wife, Sarah. They were united as one and became the owners of much wealth not because they were talented with skill but because Father God blessed them for their commitment to Him and to each other. Read in Genesis to learn about their lifestyle. Below is an example of faith shared by them as a unit.

> *4 So Abram (Abraham) left, as the Lord had told him; and Lot went with him. Abram was seventy-five years old when he set out from Haran. 5 He took his wife Sarai (Sarah), his nephew Lot, all the possessions they had accumulated and the people they had acquired in Hara, and they set out for the land of Canaan, and they arrived there. Genesis 12:4-5 NIV*

A union where a commitment has been stated by a license and a contract is sacred in the eyes of God. When one erases this stance and replaces it with a new desire, it is not honoring to the King. A second marriage, by default, is seen as a witness to faith, but integrity is shallow in form. It can still represent a sacred union, but it stands as second best. Many find themselves forced into the legal loss through a divorce. God serves them as His own too. All people fall into the category of children of the Most High. Who we represent is what is seen by God. If you have taken the step and committed adultery, you can still be redeemed. All sin can be washed clean by repentance and seeking forgiveness. A lifestyle of repeated offenses is what sets apart the lost from the true believer. Walk in the testimony of good character. Remember, others follow the lead of those in front of them. Many lean into the person who admits their sin but have turned from it in faith. A testimony can contain falls and hardships. It is where one places their heart and how they support the King that matters. Sin will no longer entice your spirit if you are truly committed to gaining hope and a forthright livelihood. You will represent the light of God, and you will lead others to the knowledge that God supports man. You won't wander around with a weight of deception because you will desire a path of good intent. God operates in the people who desire His way of life for themselves.

The pain from a loss can build and seem overwhelming. One can become confused and feel forsaken. Fear can set in and cause an envelope of agony. Many times, an income that doesn't meet the needs brings one to a place of fear where actions become devastating. Stepping in the knowledge God can bring wealth even to those with little means gives one a secure trust where God is first in the heart. A step in the right direction can bring clarity, and a whole new outlook can ensue. God opens doors and brings gifts in many forms. Someone who trusts the King begins to understand that walking in favor of faith carries the heart and mind to a plateau of unity. God understands the needs of His people, and He can develop a path that leads to a gain that wasn't a vision but now is centered in the mind. It can be an understanding or a desire to build in a manner that has new life. God can manifest a plan and create the way forward where man cannot. He works for the good, and He will lead with clear management. Hold fast to the truth that the Father is a provider. His goodwill is always on the move. He plants and breeds in a manner that showers the heart with a pathway of good form. Know the Savior is on standby and always available to hear a prayer. Your heart is known to Him. Pour out your desire and watch for an answer to come by way of good intent. God will deliver in unity that sheds hope and builds character. You won't have deception intruding, nor will there be darkness present. God brings light and gain. He is always faithful. Pursue His name and call out to Him in faith. Guidance will ensue, and you will gain a clear perspective on how to operate and where to step.

Look at how the Lord operated with His goal of building faith in His people of Israel. God offered a plan for a new home where the harvest was good and plentiful. His goal was for man to learn His good care and support; however, the people of Israel lost their way. They fell victim to the way of the deception. They desired for more meat, like was present when they lived in Egypt. In turn, this brought the curse that none of them would see the promised land other than Caleb and Joshua. Moses was only able to peer at the land, but he never set foot upon its ground. Read below how losing faith brings devastation rather than growth.

The Lord said to Moses and Aaron:

27 How long will this wicked community grumble against me? I have heard the complaints of these grumbling Israelites. 28 So tell them, 'As surely as I live, declares the Lord, I will do to you the very things I heard you say: 29 In this desert your bodies will fall-every one of you twenty years old or more who counted in the census and who has grumbled against me. 30Not one of you will enter the land I swore with uplifted hand to make your home, except Caleb son of Jephunneh and Joshua son of Nun. 31 As for your children that you said would be taken as plunder, I will bring them in to enjoy the land you have rejected. 32 But you- your bodies will fall in this desert. 33 Your children will be shepherds here for forty years, suffering for your unfaithfulness, until the last of your bodies lies in the desert. 34 For forty years-one year for each of the forty days you explored the land-you will suffer for your sins and know what it is like to have me against you.' 35 I, the Lord, have spoken, and I will surely do these things to this whole wicked community, which has banded together against me. Numbers 14:26-35 NIV

Jesus is life everlasting. He can build a bridge and offer shelter for your war-torn heart. When you aspire to the care God offers, you lean into the way He operates. Good will blossom and grow in ways you can embrace. God will engage with your heart, and you will recognize the truth of His person as that of a warrior who conquers all hardship. God invests His offering when a guided light brings clarity. This happens when an individual puts forth trust. This creates unity and the desire for faithful patronage. God will adhere to your heart and bring about a wrapping of true endearment to bind the negative pain and replace it with unity and grace. God can offer you a healing where your mind contains the knowledge of the injury, but your heart no longer processes it as a harvest of loss. You will feel uplifted with a union with the Most High. This will result in a growth where your heart and mind form a bond of glue that seals the onslaught and brings it new coverage. You won't rush into the dark desire for revenge, nor will you think on depravity. In its place will rest the peace and calm of a gentle healing that supports the work of Christ within you—his piercing on the cross-shed righteousness and purity for all of mankind. You are not an exception. You are a child He is endeared to. He loves your person and protects your inner being with knowledge that supports His character. When you claim the truth of God's Bible, you build a righteous way of being. This brings a clear mental stance of good character resulting in favor from God Himself.

Message Three

God Will Teach Mankind How to Love and Grow in Faith

He is the Waymaker

The Lord, thy God, supports man when he operates with Him in mind. Bounty is had when a heart accepts the will of the Lord. A builder needs reproof if a fault has occurred. In this manner, the option for a do-over may appear where hope and light are found. If you have an injury that needs healing, bind yourself to the will of the Father. You will gain understanding, light will shine within you, and others will learn by your example. Testing fate is not a wise way of thinking. It brings to the table a loss because the heart will fold upon itself when strangled by fear or unrest. If you favor the life of lavish living, think about the will of God and how it is applicable to that lifestyle. If you are wealthy and have abundant allowances, thank the Lord for your good gain. If you are upheld and secure in unity with the King, you will invest and profit others with your assets. You don't have to surrender all you own to be loved by God. Think about where your heart lies and whom you serve. Sink into the understanding that you are planted in a position of power in some form or another. God gifts all people with wealth of some kind. How we give to others is seen as heartfelt support or our decline. God builds upon faith. Do you support the Most High in His relationship goals with other people? Do you walk with unity so others may gain in the way of being blessed by your hand? God delivers to you a special set of circumstances that allow for growth. If you bend the bar of gratitude and launch into the desire to share your wealth, whether it be gold or an ability of some kind, God will supply the need and craft you as a caretaker and supporter.

God's unity is skilled and perfected by the hand of love. Each gold bond He forms has beauty and a forthright manner of good intent. God can bring into play the absolute way of being that supports His person. Have you written a logbook or dined on good food? An expression of gratitude can be a light to the feet of a lost person in pain and bring about a venture of opportune mementos that gift the spirit with unity. The shoulder of the Most High is elegant and fruitful. God builds with purpose, and He supports those who invest in others. He does not require a gold mine to support man.

A simple look of love toward the goal of unity is all that is needed—many support man in different forms. Our employment gifts us with clear, memorable drives that lead to bonding and creating a harvest where the mind and the goal are one. With the thought process of gaining for the sake of wealth, one loses the main concern of the heart. God leads us to a better way of presenting the truth. The Bible hosts insight and support that can bring a person to the ledge of great understanding where the heart and mind operate with care. God has a goal for all of mankind to know Him personally. This requires a plan of action detailed with an outward expression of faith led by prayer and support for King Jesus. God's gift of His Son was bestowed to us so we could gain entry to the Most High, Father God. This offering is the greatest love shown to man for all time. Even though many do not believe Jesus came in the flesh, it does not negate the truth He did. There is power to be had in admitting Jesus is who He claimed to us to be. Each direct correlation of man to God shares this truth.

God, the Father, is subtle in His care. He is direct, and He supports our hearts with love. God offers all of mankind the opportunity to perform in His good name. Some choose this path with a willing manner, while others feel stifled. If you have a nitch where your heart responds to the good offered by the Lord's hand, you have complete honest form happening. God leads and instructs in the manner of a righteous God. He does not impose or stifle one's perspective. However, if you turn from all of God's offerings only to pursue your own way, you will end up living a lie. There won't be good unity with the King, and you will have missed the love and gain God had waiting for you. An injury brings one into the light, and through the process of the pain, one can administer knowledge if truth is what they chase. God operates will skills and uniformity. Everyone gains knowledge in some form or another, and all have had some type of pain. Whether it be heartache or inflicted physical damage, pain is present at one point or other. God brings into the arena a way to heal. He grants others to administer through the prayer chain or perhaps a simple visit in the company of faith where truth is shared and love is offered. Learning the goal of unity brings the thought there is a reprieve, which brings hope to the horizon. God shoulders the desire to pursue Him in faith, and this, in turn, brings the mind to a place of rest.

Look to God and find a hope that doesn't compare to any other. Healing of the heart comes when God is pursued with faith in a trusting manner. If you believe God is a caretaker and supporter of your heart, you will entrust your walk-in life to His way of being. Look at the way God offered a life of beauty to the first children He created. See the manner they chose to defile that gift. All of mankind is fallen. Not one person would escape a life without sin compounded in their livelihood.

Now the Lord God had planted a garden in the east, in Eden; and there he put the man he had formed. 9 And the Lord God made all kinds of trees grow out of the ground-trees that were pleasing to the eye and good for food. In the middle of the garden were the tree of life and the tree of knowledge of good and evil. Genesis 1:8-9 NIV

The Lord God took the man and put him in the Garden of Eden to work it and take care of it. 16 And the Lord God commanded the man, "You are free to eat from any tree in the garden; 17 but you must not eat from the tree of the knowledge of good and evil, for when you eat of it you will surely die." Genesis 1:15-17 NIV

Now the serpent was more crafty than any of the wild animals the Lord God had made. He said to the woman, "Did God really say, 'You must not eat from any tree in the garden'?" 2 The woman said to the serpent, "We may eat fruit from the trees in the garden, but God did say, "You must not eat fruit from the tree that is in the middle of the garden, and you must not touch it, or you will die." 4 You will not surely die," the serpent said to the woman. 5 "For God knows that when you eat of it your eyes will be opened, and you will be like God, knowing good and evil." 6When the woman saw that the fruit of the tree was good for food and pleasing to the eye, and also desirable for gaining wisdom, she took some and ate it. She also gave some to her husband, who was with her, and he ate it. 7 Then the eyes of both of them were opened, and they realized they were naked; so they sewed fig leaves together and made coverings for themselves. Genesis 3:1-7 NIV

Testing the Lord God brings man out of the will of the Father. One will lose solid footing and step into a path of loss. God builds when we work with His favor. This happens when we apply our heart and mind to build a better relationship with His person. If you invest time with the King, He, in turn, will grant you wisdom and truth, as this is how he imparts knowledge to our hearts. God builds us with favor when we acknowledge Him as our supporter and Waymaker. The King of man is ever at our side. We need only to impart our thought process toward His way of being, and we gain a united bond where we are joined to God in unity and care. God offers all of mankind the way to know Him personally through the blood of His Son Jesus. The cross was the ultimate gift to mankind. It is the gateway to gaining freedom and leaning into the Savior. If you believe Jesus is who He claims He is, then you realize God is the utmost High being. He alone is the one to craft our hearts and build us in His image. He works for the good of man. He is always pursuing mankind as He is the Father to us all. God favors no one above another, but He does offer favor to those who are faithful. God is always forthright and giving in the manner of faith and hope. He grants these two giftings freely. One needs only to pray and impart love upon the Savior, and growth will happen.

The unity God offers is right with an abundant way of gain. He supplies the needed measure where a heart drives the needed truth and unveils the love of God. Following in faith is the support required for man to achieve a bounty that speaks of beauty and fruit. When the power of faith enters a scene, man gains in the manner of good, moral hygiene. A growing embodiment of faith ensues when a person reads the Word of God and applies it to his way of life. Without working toward the goal of unification with God, a heart will not mend. A pain of injury found within the barrier of the mind grows weary when no fruit is had.

A stand of unity in the righteous manner of truth is what allows a person to grow in a spiritual way of being. The one who claims truth is God alone. He is the only one who can plant a union where the mind is healed alongside the progress of gaining trust where God and you are joined. It doesn't require a formal request, just a simple expression of favor to Christ, and a union will be created. The Father of all mankind is supportive in the way of a true witness of love. No other is as kind or supportive, nor can there be but one true Savior. Jesus is the reason man exists. It is because of His willing expression of unity that man can know Him personally. The labor of love He put forth was a unifying measure no man can compare to. God alone is the great I Am. The beauty of knowing Jesus brings to light true unity. There is no conflict or misdirection. Only the right cause of truth is heard when the Savior is who you follow. The Father of man is not hollow or light in His makeup. He is pure unity and love. He represents the goal of light and stands as a superior, right justified being.

The stance of God is always one of faith and support. These are His life-giving qualities. He is compact and built with total, glorious manners that always lead man in the direction of care. One who finds favor with God is gifted the way ahead where all He claims will be witnessed to. God leads and cares for man in a manner no other comprehends. His unity and form of righteousness lead in a sure-footed mode of light. The way a man should invest is discovered on the pages of the Bible. Many verses speak of God's care and union. Look at one example below. It will speak truth to your heart and breathe into you a longing to know the Savior in a better way.

By this time it was late in the day, so his disciples came to him. "This is a remote place," they said, "and it's already very late. 36 Send the people away so they can go to the surrounding countryside and villages and buy themselves something to eat." 37 But he answered, "you give them something to eat." They said to him, "That would take eight months of a man's wages! Are we to go and spend that much on bread and give it to them to eat?" 38 "How many loaves do you have?" he asked. "Go and see." When they found out, they said, "Five- and two fish." 39 Then Jesus directed them to have all the people sit down in groups on the green grass. 40 So they sat down in groups of hundreds and fifties. 41 Taking the five loaves and the two fish and looking up to heaven, he gave thanks, and broke the loaves. Then he gave them to his disciples to set before the people. He also divided the two fish among them all. 42 They all ate and were satisfied, 43 and the disciples picked up twelve basketfuls of broken pieces of bread and fish. 44 The number of the men who had eaten was five thousand. Mark 6:35-44 NIV

Look at where faith has secured your heart and mind. Were you alone, or did you feel the presence of the Most High? Were you capable of moving forward on a plan, or did you enlist another's aid? God operates with care and support and never steps outside of a just cause. If you believe the Lord is faithful, determine for yourself that God can bring you to a place of beauty where your heart and mind focus on Him alone. When this transpires, a new pathway unfolds, and a perspective of good moral conduct ensues. God is the giver of good judgment. In Him, one attains the unity and the balance of true insight that supports the goal of life where mind and body are complete. A way ahead is seen as good when God is the goal setter. You can't obtain a union where God is first if you look outside His Word for unity. God's Word supports who God is as a person. The great I Am is a leader and a standard that surpasses all understanding. Man can attempt to gain immortality, but he will fail and lose his way. Only when we walk in a justified manner does true integrity come into view. God is our anchor, and our stance needs to reflect Him.

Look at where God has placed His unity. His Son was gifted to all for the sake of knowing the Lord in a personal way. This shows how important we are to Him. The sacrifice of Jesus on the cross-bore witness that the Savior is all knowing, and we are the apple of His eye. God understood man would fail on all levels, so He crafted a way for man to enter the grace of His unity. This happened when Jesus shed His blood that day at Calvary. The story of God revealing to His children how to gain entry to His person can be read in the following verses.

> ***"For God so loved the world that he gave his one and only Son, that whoever believes in him shall not perish but have eternal life. 17 For God did not send his Son into the world to condemn the world, but to save the world through him. John 3:16-17 NIV***

The Lord is always steadfast and righteous. Through His way of presenting faith to the heart, man gains the bounty of trust. This brings to the forefront a way of great hope to be manifested. If a person has the understanding God is with them on a personal level, they lean into the knowledge God is at work on their behalf. God is always a Waymaker. He organizes the heart and gifts it with trust. God considers how to perform in a personal arena where His heart is tied to the individual calling on His name. God can bring to life a solid bond that offers the heart a real connection. If you have an injury and are in need of aid, God can bring to light the direct way to proceed so you are better equipped to move in a solid, foundational process creating a desired verdict for the heart to flourish. Even when there is injury, God lifts the burden and carries the cure to the mind, where love can manifest and grow. All the hurt brought on by stress in a marriage is removed if Jesus is the one pursued. God has a bounty for the one who invests in His care and support. The unity found in this experience is a gain of instruction that provides the heart and mind with good, moral conduct. A lie will not breed if trust is put forth toward the King and His way of being is put forward. Look toward the unity found in the Word of God. Many passages reflect how God felt about His people, the Israelites. He cared for them even though they fought against Him with their pursual of false gods. God always stayed by their side and brought good care to their hearts.

Discipline was often injected upon them to right their course of action so they would better know the way to tread. God always brings the hand of love even through the rod of strength when the goal of unity is at work. We often want to leave a gap where doubt enters, and we feel at ease in wallowing. We enjoy the presence of justification even if it stays on the exterior of good intent. Following in the way of unity will align our thought process and lead us toward the goal of a true witness and good behavior. God is the way to exist as a whole. It is His manners that align us to quality thinking and actions. When the Lord is our goal, our thoughts join His mental process, and we invest in the wisdom that supports our bond. The unity the cross brought is justified and wholesome. If ever there were a reason to trust in Jesus, the day He shed His blood for mankind should reflect the true grafting God had in mind for His people to be joined to His person.

The light of the cross shines bright as Jesus is the honorary being that framed the heart of man in the will of the Father. The God of heaven and earth never fails, nor does He falter. His walk is true and supports the goal of building in a manner of faith that exudes love and care. When God is at the helm of a build, you are guaranteed a solid foundational structure where the heart and mind are tied to purity. God builds in a manner of good intent. He is structurally sound, and all He created is a barricade of bright integrity. A call may come to your spirit where you desire a goal that is outside of the scope of your ability. Trust God to deliver a way ahead. If you find a standstill transpires, believe God has a plan, and it will happen in due time according to a steadfast lean and suit of authorship where all components are justified with care. God delivers on a goal in the precise manner that best builds the goal He put forth. Waiting can be a trial, so look to God and His Word for comfort. It will raise obedience that supports the structure of the build even though no understanding is present for moving ahead at the moment of the wait. Should a unity be in need, lean into God for care. He will provide the vision for more stance, and you will learn the goal of His intent. Not all builds happen in a day. Think about Nehemiah and the building of the wall around Jerusalem. It took many hands and much labor before the final draft was in place. Read below for insurance concerning this gift placed at the throne of God once completion happened.

At the dedication of the wall of Jerusalem, the Levites were sought out from where they lived and were brought to Jerusalem to celebrate joyfully the dedication with songs of thanksgiving and with the music of cymbals, harps, and lyres. 28 The singers also were brought together from the region around Jerusalem-from

the villages of the Netophathites, 29 from Beth Gilgal, and from the area of Geba and Azmaveth, for the singers had built villages for themselves around Jerusalem. 30 When the priests and Levites had purified themselves ceremonially, they purified the people, the gates and the wall. Nehemiah 12:27-30 NIV

Look at how God can build so much for man and yet be without the care of his heart. This points to the love God holds within. Man often forgets who the great I Am is and walks outside of good form. God does not leave the side of man; instead, He instills the desire to know Him better. It is up to the individual as to whether he invests in the knowledge God puts forth. Many believe they are wise, but they do not understand true commitment or gain. Many have acquired wealth that supports the bank statement without caring about how the union of God to man exists. In the long-term, man will never know real unity until he admits Jesus is the way to life ever after. Without this knowledge, there is no purpose in compiling an account of wealth as it will all rust and decay away. What stands the test of time is wealth, like God. If you invest in man and his needs, this serves as fresh where God ordains your investment and feeds it character. No one individual can obtain a bond of true clarity without reading the Word of the Bible. This is God's ordained witness with proof of ownership in the pages of truth.

People need this instruction to be able to materialize a faith-based way of proceeding in life. Never assume God has taken you under His wing if you are building through theft or deceit. God does not support this behavior, and He will topple all that is acquired in this manner. The builder of intent must realize God is the one in control. He is the one who can bring the gift of grace, which brings a salve to any misfortune or structure of loss. Grace also brings a bond of good intent where unity is subject to the power of God. If God is at the back of all you put forth, there will not be solid, foundational network allowances to your structure of support. He must reside as the utmost, valued being in your heart and mind.

The reason man does not gain in the way of unity is tied to the fact he is not operating in trust with the Lord. If a wayward gain takes form, it will not adhere for the long term, so that the investment will be lost. Look at where your heart responds when a call to submit to the Most High is presented. Are you offering your skill level to those in need, or is there always a price tag adjoined to your work? Where is the leadership set you have obtained? Does it rest in the arm of God, or are you looking for recognition and fame? God may gift one with an important title, but this doesn't mean a vast knowledge of unity is in play. God has favor when work is reputable and forthright. He brings a clear mental gain that supports His way of being. Through the growth network of His love, man can better adhere to the bond of care presented as a leadership quality. God caters to the man who relishes His strength and leans into Him with unity. When a person rotates and yields a vast horizon of good, moral being, multiple ways of growth unfold. What measures as wholesome depends on where the heart was led and how it applied the will of the Father in its pursuit of gain. Bounty comes forward when hope and a stance of purity find a home within the heart and mind. A beautiful undertaking ensues when a person operates with these as a motive.

God is the main expression of love, and following His commands offers a heart great integrity where love and honest form can combine as a unit of opportunity. Each detail of the guard can bring to light a manner of true character if the Lord is the focus for each step. The pursual of the Most High leads one in the direction of good care. Binding the heart toward the union of God will encapsulate a person in a care unit that supports all of man, and his manner will express true gain for many. If you are hoping to better know how to build a heart of pure intent, look toward the strength of Noah when the flood was to come and destroy the earth. He built, not knowing when the first drop of rain would fall. That showed he understood the Lord and knew He was supporting the goal of Noah to have comfort when the storm came.

So God said to Noah, "I am going to put an end to all people, for the earth is filled with violence because of them. I am surely going to destroy both them and the earth. 14 So make yourself an ark of cypress wood; make rooms in it and coat it with pitch inside and out. 15 This is how you are to build it: The ark is to be 450 feet long, 75 feet wide and 45 feet high. 16 Make a roof for it and finish the ark to within 18 inches of the top. Put a door in the side

of the ark and make lower, middle and upper decks. 17 I am going to bring floodwaters on the earth to destroy all life under the heavens, every creature that has the breath of life in it. Everything on earth will perish. 18 But I will establish my covenant with you, and you will enter the ark-you and your sons and your wife and your son's wives with you, 19 You are to bring into the ark two of all living creatures, male and female, to keep them alive with you. 20 Two of every kind of bird, of every kind of animal and of every kind of creature that moves along the ground will come to you to be kept alive, 21 You are to take every kind of food that is to be eaten and store it away as food for you and for them," 22 Noah did everything just as God commanded him. Genesis 6:13-22 NIV

The Lord delivers the heart instruction which manifests and portrays a unity where the heart knows the King personally even though no investment has been in play. God has designed man to engage with Him on an intimate level. If this isn't transpiring in your relationship goal with God, you are not being wise in your daily walk. A lead by the hand of God will enact a bounty that is rich and savoring with pure standing. God justifies the heart and makes it aware of a dark presence. This produces good intent and sets an example of righteous endeavors. When God is at the helm a way of life leading to good conduct will manifest and bloom. A tailgate of length will abound in the manner of an acceptance that God is the genuine one of faith. The power of the written Word is made complete by the hand of God. He crafted each paragraph and each display of trust presented on the pages therein known as the Bible. This gift supports the knowledge God is the all in all.

The written unity one gains from the Book of knowledge is forever a gain and stature of uncompromising good care. The pages reflect truth and support the King for who He truly is. The knowledge God is abundant in His faith and teaching of love grants the unity tied to the man who invests in reading and learning the messages of every scripture detail planted in the stream of righteous, moral leadership. God has planted His heart within the Book to better enlighten man to His person. We have power in our hands when we apply our hearts and minds to embracing the words of the Bible. Scripture feeds the spirit, and it enables us to fight the enemy of the dark world known as Satan. Satan has no power outside of influence or inflicting pain in the form of lies and deceit. It can be easy to fall prey to deception if you aren't preparing yourself in the way of scripture protection on a regular basis. The knowledge found in the bonded words gifts one with a coverage where the heart and mind form a barrier against the intrusion of the enemy of God. Following the leadership of the Lord benefits the body on a whole which builds bounty and transforms a person for the better in his display of personal traits.

The teaching of the Word to people comes by way of trained unity with God the Father. This is the result of following faithfully the King, the great I Am. God the Father is united with His Son Jesus. The two work as one and both are caregivers and supporters of the human race. God created man in His image thus relating to him in a personal manner. When you think about the care God offers to man a realization of the Most High becomes clear. God is wise and holy. He never brings doubt or a loss to the heart. When one invests in the manner of unity with God an envelope of love unfolds. God has through all of time been faithful and supportive to His people known as the bride of Christ. You can bank on the fact God will never harm you when you walk the path of faith and trust. Leading in the manner of doubt will only bring a case of loss. If you apply toward the goal of building a bond where your heart and mind grow in the direction of God you will gain in the way of hope. Alongside will come a bounty that represents good precepts and thought processes. God is the delight of man when unity is present. God builds a support measure when a person leans into His personal instruction found written on the pages of love and hope ensues. For some this proves to be a strain but the ones who pursue God in love find life everlasting. God the Father grants insight to a believer that escapes the heart of someone who turns away from the bond presented. If you have lost a love and now choose to forget them as an individual, you can relate to what transpires when someone rejects the love of God. No unity is supported, and no harvest of good intent ever is brought forth. Caring about people brings light to the heart and an authority of righteous manner comes forward. God builds a bond when a person invites Him into his life and leaves a window of light for God to manifest within. Our hearts are made to know the Lord. If we pursue the King, the unity is fed, and gain is always available. The God of man is forthright. He never abducts a person against his will. If you desire to know the Lord invite Him to pursue you in faith. The trust you need will grow and prayer will bring to light the truth of the Savior and His good way. Our lives matter to God. Never doubt Jesus is waiting for you to know Him better.

A look at scripture gifts the heart and mind with clear mental gain. It builds the heart and supports the goal of the Father to know Him personally. Let's invest in this process by reading and applying the goal of love toward God.

> *Delight yourself in the Lord and he will give you the desires of your heart. 5 Commit your way to the Lord; trust in him and he will do this: 6 He will make your righteousness shine like the dawn, the justice of your cause like the noonday sun. Psalm 37:4-6 NIV*

Believe the Lord God is ever faithful. By unifying your heart with the knowledge God is a Waymaker you will learn the support He offers is always available. When pain is present God can bring a salve where your mind gains love in place of deception. A person whose marriage has been washed away due to infidelity often lives in a bitter tangle of hate. The personal manner of betrayal causes one to feel inadequate alongside that of fear and the two deceptive thought processes bring a bounty of deceit to the heart. Looking at how God deals with rejection enlightens the mind as to who to serve and how to proceed in faith. A love quest feeds the mind with care and that is who the Savior our God is to His people. If your heart leans on the truth of the great I Am it gains the bounty of restored growth and soon the fear or rejection becomes a mere loss of time in place of an injury that festers. An infection causes the body to become ill. This factor happens with bitterness as well. When the spirit feels slighted, and it manufactures the insult into a growth of hate bitterness takes root and mental anguish is brought forward. This in turn drives the mind to revenge causing injury to the inner being alongside of the physical presentation that it represents to others. People on the outside of the party involved with the dissolving of a marriage witness the loss and feel the injured parties wound. They in turn will either build upon the rejected statement or they will pursue the King for a manifestation of truth. Faith comes to the person who believes God is supportive and giving in His person. The Bible represents who the Father is to man. God has gifted us with the intent of knowing Him in a personal manner so harvest this authorship and gain a unity of clear understanding and support.

> *If the Lord delights in a man's way, he makes his steps firm; 24 though he stumble, he will not fall, for the Lord upholds him with his hand. Psalm 37:23-24 NIV*

God favors a man who invests in the goal of building in faith the support of mankind. If you apply your efforts toward the growth of another individual God will support this activity and breed into it more gain. The support of the heart is made clear when the offering of help comes by way of mentoring and leading others into the light of who God is. Your actions can speak truth simply by representing faith in the manner of good care. Our opportunity to witness is portrayed in the form of servanthood. Caring for the life of someone who has no wealth that will benefit you directly shows a true love for mankind. This is how the Lord enables His people to better equip one another in the way of good mental gain. Have you thought about the way man breached the wall of deceit when he accepted Jesus as the true Messiah? Many understand the knowledge of God because faith has been applied and intent was given in pure faith. People who lean into the Savior know Him on a personal level thus resulting in the gain of unity where hope comes to life as a whole. God's support manifests and breeds life into the heart of anyone willing to trust His directive. You may operate without the source of power known as God's will, but it won't breathe life into your soul. Only God can bring this quality of good form to your spirit.

God is the one who invented good care. It is by His manner that we learn and grow in wisdom and support for one another. The path of lighted understanding is found in the pages of God's support Book, the Bible. Look at the verse of unity God composed in the scripture below. God will support you when you do.

"Be still, and know that I Am God; I will be exalted among the nations, I will be exalted in the earth." 11 The Lord Almighty is with us; the God of Jacob is our fortress. Psalm 46:10-11 NIV

God works in the favor of man as a unit of faith is made manifest. When a viewpoint conflicts with the Father it will not blossom or grow in the manner of good intent. If you apply a goal of purity no ill repute will enter into the union of harmony God puts forth. The love of the Father is a binding factor that supports the heart and provides it with grace. This bounty is supportive and manifests great bonding. The love of the Most High is offered to all of mankind. God does not discriminate or favor one person over another. He offers to all His love and care. It is by His goodwill that man is able to know Him and to secure a righteous manner that presents a walk of harmony. With God there is never a slight or infringement unless the individual seeks to gain outside of the good knowledge God offers him. God is abundant with His offering of love. He provides man with grace, and this is what establishes the core of the relationship. If you desire to plant a return, look at the way God operates. With this knowledge one can build a great mile of true intent. God has established the manner for man to walk and He knows the best way forward. Believe in the power God is capable of and know God brings light and truth to any endeavor.

Greed causes many to fall and as a result man leaves the nest of true warranty. God's home is an example of purity not deceit. God will always plan a build where man will harvest fruit that supports good, moral character. God showers a person with understanding if prayer is a part of his life. This brings about a connection where unity is formed, and grace takes form of the manifested union. God offers man hope with gain in the manner of good intent. This transforms the heart and offers it a reprieve in the event a hardship was inflicted. Even the life of a beggar can shine hope if God is known to them in a personal manner. Who God works through can be anyone of any standing. He does not discriminate. Education is not a factor when God is on the move. A degree is not what determines the height of the goal God builds upon. If you suffer from knowledge deficit don't fall victim to the lie you aren't valuable. God can use you just as you are.

Many believe a walk with God is difficult but when in reality it is very simple in form. Satan leads many astray in this area. Walking with the Savior shines as an example when a person is forthright and meaningful when they correspond with one another. Honesty needs to always be the marker of your thought process.

Build upon it and bake in the great opportunities that come alongside this way of living. Being a person of character determines the ground you are supported by. God does not walk where weeds grow in the spirit. He rests with the heart that invites in purity and honest form.

Message Four

God Will Bring to Light
When a Heart is in Need of Salvation

He speaks in a clear and thought-provoking manner

God works to support man as He loves the creation He built. Man is God's child, and He loves him dearly. If you are a parent, you can relate to this understanding. The goal of God is to have a relationship with man that leads to eternal life. The way of hope comes from the Father, who invests His care as a reward that benefits man's heart. All the gifting God manifests into the heart is bounty by His hand alone. No one can bring the beauty God has within His person to another in the manner God supplies. We are gifted with talent and spiritual guidance components, but this is too part of God's representative way of being. Our goal should be to reflect the King and look at Him as our guidance counselor. Each graft God applies to our person is good and supportive of Him in nature. Reading the Bible brings to light the truth of the nature of God. Every scripture verse reflects the love of the Most High. Below is an example of true manifested grace.

> *God is our refuge and strength, an ever-present help in trouble.*
> *Psalm 46:1 NIV*

The Savior of mankind always follows the bar of truth. He builds the stance of good, moral conduct and engages with others in a manner of good intent. You can know Him personally by embracing Him as your Lord. You can gain wisdom through the witness He offers, written in the Book of enlightenment. God offers His heart on His sleeve when you engage in reading scripture and applying your mindset to its presence of truth. If you fail in your daily walk, reading the Lord's words will aid you. No one can walk without applying their heart to the Word of God regularly. Favor is granted when man adjusts his heart to the acceptance that God is who He claims to be. Reading the Bible infiltrates the mind with the revelation of truth and how to strive toward the goal of bonded union with the Most High, the great I Am. To venture out onto a cliff proves foolish if guard rails are not in place. A fall could ensue, and life could be lost.

God offers the rail of justice where a heart dines on the luxury of opportune growth, which supports the mind with clear mental gain. Understanding God operates in a realm man does not comprehend relays the truth God is superior to man in all ways that present as good.

God the Father manifests love to all of mankind. When a person needs to find faith, a simple profession toward the Most High brings a clear mental gain that supports the person of Jesus. This is what manifests a bond and forms a union. God, the Father, hears our claim that Jesus is real and supports our hearts with pure intent. We lean into the way of the Master, and growth begins to expand in the manner of true knowledge with a focus on God. Our time in the Word organizes our minds and brings support from the hand of God. The written Bible is a complete unit in prayer and the goal of unity designed by God Himself. Look at how man is able to learn about Jesus by reading the Book of love. Every verse is a mainframe of love and a gift of support. If you long to meet the Savior and are struggling with the way to bring this in alignment with your person, take time to read scripture. It will enlighten your eyes, and your heart will expand. You will gain unity with God, and your eyesight will be enhanced. A clear vision will ensue, and an understanding will begin to form. The knowledge of the Word is a gift from above.

God is our refuge and strength, an ever-present help in trouble. Psalm 46:1 NIV

A witness is produced when a heart embraces the truth of the Word and presents it to another. Our belief reflects our good intent. Actions that bind the love of God to another are a simple quest all are able to expand upon. In some situations, people build by serving another with food or shelter. This is an example that many have offered by sharing their home. Reading a book and then offering to others the knowledge you found is another example of how to care for someone other than yourself. Selfless acts of support are what bring others to the saving knowledge of God. It is by offering care and support that man entertains kings and laymen. Both are important and support one another by way of leadership. Many find sharing the Gospel rewarding and a blessing, while others are intimidated by doing so. You aren't required to be a scholar. You simply need to understand the message of the cross. Anyone, rich or poor, can tell a story of good form. God's leadership within our hearts is what sends the truth to the mind of a friend or family member. An acquaintance can be enlightened by gifting him with a card or note. There is not one particular angle to present. Do an action that speaks of your character or way of being. Discover hope in the process and build unity with the King. Many achieve the level of pastor or minister, but not all people are designed to witness in this manner. Trust Jesus to gift you with talent that supports the person you are. He will lead you with a goal, and a beautiful bounty will shine.

The goal of man is to share with others the knowledge he gains. If a person is led to interact with another, it may result in a path of unity that entertains both parties and directs the mind to a partnership. Being led to invest in a dream can create a bond between two people with the same intent. God may deem investing in a path where another is front and center is important. This does not mean you aren't important to the gift of union God bound together. It is a measure of leadership that stands as a unit. Many desire to know where they should invest or lead in the community. God will open doors and offer a path in the direction of good intent while investing in you as a person. Your talent will reveal how best to serve others, and this will align with a building that rests on the name of the Lord. God works in the lives of the willing. Each bounty you hold in your hand has been in support of favor toward a goal of accomplishment. However, if you have built with care and a learned endeavor of supporting the Most High, you have gained in the way of unity. God operates with care and gifts those who desire a walk of faith with His person. If you build outside of structure and importance, you walk the line of loss. God brings truth to all He manifests. Build in truth and love, so it spans the dense years. A path of good, moral conduct will far surpass the length of a negative desire. With God, beauty springs forth, and opportunity is planted with no shame involved in the process. The length of any transforming option and the goal of good intent takes time.

Understand God works for the end game of greatness. He does not build in haste, nor does He rush a process. The care He invests toward a union where bounty is to be had will align with good form. God is always righteous and fair. Trust His leadership and Know God loves you through the work endeavor. The work of man is complex if an engineer is needed for the blueprint to take shape. But even the simplest build can involve the heart of man and be important to many. God operates in a manner of great strength. Let Him guide your process and grow with His person as your instructor.

God is a caretaker and a support person of love. If you have an injury needing gain, look at how God healed the leper.

A man with leprosy came to him and begged him on his knees, "If you are willing, you can make me clean." 41 Filled with compassion, Jesus reached out his hand and touched the man. "I am willing," he said, "Be clean!" 42 Immediately the leprosy left him and he was cured. Mark 1:40-41 NIV

God supports man, and He advises him with care. God never extinguishes the heart but brings it to the light. God will craft within man the goal of a union where the Lord directs the heart and mind. Look at the way God operated within the guidance of Solomon. God made Solomon wise, and He gifted him with much wealth.

Your servant is here among the people you have chosen, a great people, too numerous to count or number. 9 So give your servant a discerning heart to govern your people and to distinguish between right and wrong. For who is able to govern this great people of yours?" 10 The Lord was pleased that Solomon had asked for this. 11 So God said to him, "Since you have asked for this and not for long life or wealth for yourself, nor have asked for the death of your enemies but for discernment in administering justice, 12 I will do what you have asked. I will give you a wise and discerning heart, so that there will never have been anyone like you, nor will there ever be. 13 Moreover, I will give you what you have not asked for-both riches and honor-so that in your lifetime you will have no equal among kings. 14 And if you walk in my ways and obey my statutes and commands as David your father did, I will give you a long life." 15 Then Solomon awoke-and he realized it had been a dream. 1Kings 3:8-15 NIV

God offers man insight with guidance. He cares and supports the goal of the heart when truth is the basis for a person's walk. God, the Father, is a caregiver in whom all of man is recognized. The leadership of God is contained within the parameter of all things good and right. God does not operate in a shadow of deceit. He will not abide in the dark. He is always light, and good form flows through His person. We can know the leadership of God will contain important measures where beauty and love are bred. God's leading guarantees us a landing of good, moral, investment characters. The leadership value God puts forth will always be a sign of purity. If you are led into the swamp, know God is not at the helm. The enemy of God operates there, and he will lead you to a loss. His aim is to destroy. He is the opposite of God. Darkness is his very being. Follow the path of bright imaginings and be led with care. If you pursue the love God offers, you will inherit a bounty that resides for all time. Time is fleeting, but life is eternal. Determine now how you spend your eternal days.

God is life and great measures of love. In Him, we are given a way ahead that builds with character and good frames. God has invested His Son for our good which is a measure of His great desire for us to know Him personally. Our time and talent are how we invest in the Lord. Look at the way man has been led to follow the Lord in the manner of faith. Abraham (Abram) is a good measure of life toward God. Below is a verse that speaks to gain God brought to Abraham (Abram). God never left his side, and He always made a way for him to be blessed.

The Lord had said to Abram, "Leave your country, your people and your father's household and go to the land I will show you. 2 I will make you into a great nation and I will bless you; I will make your name great, and you will be a blessing. 3 I will bless

those who bless you, and whoever curses you I will curse; and all peoples on earth will be blessed through you. Genesis 12:1-3 NIV

God lifts the spirit, and He embellishes the heart with good form. Believing God cares for you shows a heart and body the will the Father contains for your person. Thinking God is good aligns the mind to the grace God has on the platform of a bond called unity. When God embraces your person, you will gain in the manner of good intent. Your thought process will begin to build in support of others, and your intent will adjust to that which is prosperous by way of growth in a manner of enlightenment that leads to a uniform presentation of good.

God offers man the ability to know Him as a person of love and hope. God is always faithful and supports man even when man leads a life of sin. God can bring a clear faith that builds light and supports the heart so truth will be revealed. If ever you desire to learn who the Father leans into, simply look to the truth of God's Word and believe in His great love. You will better realize the foundation of trust, enabling you to gain in the manner of great wealth. Man's wealth is not the same as that of the Most High. With God, bounty is valued as a pure way of being and a manner of love and faith toward His person. God operates for the better of man. He provides love and support that represents His character and reveals the spirit of His guidance.

In the same manner, walking with the King Jesus builds the heart and mind toward the goal of unity where love resides. If ever a doubt enters your thought process, lean into the truth provided in the Bible. All passages are true and right. There is not one mistake in the Word of God. All scripture is by the Master's hand, so it is correct and true. It supports the person of the Lord, so you gain truth and honor through spiritual knowledge. God leads with purpose, and He invests in His people with care. He grafts to the heart of man an understanding that leads to good, moral, right thinking. You can build unity if you apply your life goal toward knowledge and let God deliver the truth. He will act with support, and you will adhere to His character with a sense of trust. God never fails, and He always lifts up. His encouragement is designed to align our hearts with His way of being. By His power, we learn and operate as He does. It is better to build with the one who created life than to trust in your own leadership and lose the gift of eternal life. God supports man when he invests in the Savior. Knowing the Lord God is the greatest investment one can decide to commit to. God is always at your side when you invite Him to walk with you in all you do in life. He comes to your aid, and He delivers faith upon request. All He supports is right and good. God is valuable in that He is the great I Am. He created all life, and He built upon the growth of leadership He manifested in the way of fruit of the heart. We are designed to reproduce in the manner of love and support.

When we follow the lead of God, we gain faith, and with that investment is found true guidance which supports the love of man for God Himself. Our mind falls short in the way of purity, but God is always wholesome and good. He is what we look to for all good things. God, the Father, is the Waymaker. He is ever close and tied to our hearts. He does not intrude upon our way of thinking but shines the light of truth in our direction. If you are in doubt as to where you're planting your life, think about the character presented in the Book of Matthew. It shines in the manner of who Jesus was and how He manifested His good care to people.

> *As Jesus went on from there, two blind men followed him, calling out, "Have mercy on us, Son of David!" 28 When he had gone indoors, the blind men came to him, and he asked them, "Do you believe that I am able to do this?" "Yes, Lord," they replied. 29 Then he touched their eyes and said, "According to your faith will it be done to you"; 30 and their sight was restored. Jesus warned them sternly, "See that no one knows about this." 31 But they went out and spread the news about him all over that region. Matthew 9:27-31 NIV*

God supports the love of Himself to the people He cares for and supports. If you have been wounded in a battle of faith and have ended up with scars and injuries, know the love God holds for you is far superior to that of man. God leads and operates with true moral gain, and He delivers the mind a clear bounty, so it is fed and embellished upon. No wound of pain can outdo the Father and His care. With God, a person can build faith and know there will be a golden and forthright return. God won't rob you, nor will you be taken advantage of. He is always honest and good in all He does. God cannot sin, so you can trust His value as solid and morally right. God breeds with love, and He never negates the work He designs. Your heart is a delight to His, and He desires it to reflect His character. He will guide your thought process, and by His person, you will know good moral thinking.

God is light, and in Him is found the reward of true character. If you believe the Lord will show you favor, He abounds with gifts to the spirit. He instructs and leads; in the process, you grow and learn how to manifest good work, which results in rewards and gain. God leads with genuine favor that breeds love and care. Money is often a builder of negativity. God can bring it to life and make it a tool that grants a life of sharing and giving so others may learn and grow. True love of man brings to the table riches alongside care and support in the way of spiritual gain. When God brings a life toward the goal of building a good verdict of unity, many prosper and learn true leadership where life is fed and supported. An injury of the heart can be healed when God is the crafter of the bounty it leans into. Many have found faith is a measure of true love, and with it comes the knowledge God cares and supports without end. Learning to embrace the Lord completely is a gift where the heart and mind adhere to truth. The love God offers is complete, and it is good. He is a gateway to beauty and plants the heart in a bounty of true care. God is real. He is a Waymaker, and through His way of being, all of mankind is made right. If you doubt the Lord can build for you as He has another, think about how God worked in the life of Job. Job lived in the care of God. God rebuilt his broken life, and He granted him a restored gain proving God is righteous and good.

After Job had prayed for his friends, the Lord made him prosperous again and gave him twice as much as he had before. Job 42:10 NIV

12 The Lord blessed the latter part of Job's life more than the first. He had fourteen thousand sheep, six thousand camels, a thousand yoke of oxen and a thousand donkeys. 13 And he also had seven sons and three daughters. 14 The first daughter he named Jemimah, the second Keziah and the third Keren-

Happuch. 15 Nowhere in all the land were there found women as beautiful as Job's daughters, and their father granted them an inheritance along with their brothers. 16 After this Job lived a hundred and forty years; he saw his children and their children to the fourth generation. 17 And so he died, old and full of years. Job 42;12-17 NIV

The God of all mankind is supportive in nature and rewards the heart and mind with unity. By His stance, man gains in the way of blessed hope. God is always available for fellowship. He supports the knowledge of good, upright manners. Through His person, one gains free access by receiving the holy King Jesus. Jesus presents man the opportunity to move ahead and gain in the manner of true intimacy by leaning into Him and letting Him guide the thought process of the mind. The stance of true, gifted peace is by the Father's hand. You can gain in the manner of wealth, but without the profession of faith, you won't find unity where you and God become one. A team of strength builds between you and He, and in the process, light is presented. A cloud of doubt may try to intrude, but with the peace of God, one can sweep it away. The gift of the bond of favor will begin to shine, and you will adhere to a stable undertaking where your heart is renewed, and you gain freedom without the pain of yesterday. Trials can build character if God is the focus of the heart. The lead of God to your person grants the desire of future atonement in that the mind is renewed with direction of surplus and gain. With God, the mind is presented a manner of true prosperity, and hope manifests where pain once labored. Look at how God operated with many of the people from scripture. His lead was always good and healthy.

I waited patiently for the Lord; he turned to me and heard my cry. 2 He lifted me out of the slimy pit, out of the mud and mire; he set my feet on a rock and gave me a firm place to stand. 3 He put a new song in my mouth, a hymn of praise to our God. Many will see and fear and put their trust in the Lord. Psalm 40:1-3 NIV

God is a multiplier of faith. If ever you are troubled or in need of hope, God will supply your heart with comfort. His Word is righteous and presents a beauty that builds the mind a tree envelope of care. When God applies the heart toward the goal of unity, a balance of perfect harmony ensues. God supports the growth of love where the heart and mind form unity and spring forward with divine sanctity. God, the Father, is a caregiver. He leads and builds in many forms. If you are planning a new career or perhaps a new marriage, think about how God can bring life to your plan. He joins where He is welcomed. If you take this to heart and offer God your thought process, you will inherit joy and support. God is the giver of life. He manifests the heart into a peaceful setting, and a peaceful bond will be built upon it. Knowing the Savior results in a relationship gifted with trust. God leads the heart and mind in the direction of His own good favor. He grafts to your spirit the love He holds, and you learn solid, moral discipleship. God is always available for instruction. His Bible is complete, so every situation has been represented. There are no gaps or holes. God has planted His guidance in such a manner that man can find support for all his goals and desires.

Robin (Rochel) Arne

Message Five

God is Righteous and True

He is bound by love and cannot sin. He is ever true

The unity God offers is stable and just. In His care, man thrives and gains a reprieve when pain has been implemented against him. The Lord garners the mind with a love that none can compare to. The Father is ever faithful and supports the bond of man to His person. God loves all of mankind. He looks at them as His children.

The connection God offers when an injury has transpired is designed to heal and bring a salve of good form. If you feel forsaken, read how God revealed to Isaiah the goal of purity, where he learned God was faithful and just.

> *10 Tell the righteous it will be well with them, for they will enjoy the fruit of their deeds. 11Woe to the wicked! Disaster is upon them! They will be paid back for what their hands have done. Isaiah 3:10-11 NIV*

The Lord is gifted with beauty and radiance of good nature. In Him is found the support and harmony where all He builds is righteous. God is absolute. God designs man as a leader of good intent, but man becomes unrighteous when he favors outside of God and His moral compass. If you have fallen short in the desire to pursue the King, remember all of mankind is sinful. Not one person is without sin. Man has sin nature, so he fails to always abide by what is good and wholesome. With God, man can be reborn. The cross is the salvation gift, which sets apart the fallen from the righteous.

Accepting Jesus as the one and only true Lord is the first step in becoming His child. The redeeming power of Christ's blood is the bridge that enables man to go from broken to saved. God offered His Son as a means to know Him better. Jesus is our Waymaker. He alone crafts the bounty that incorporates the heart in care and grants it operational goodness. Jesus never sinned even though He came to earth as a man. He was fully God incarnate just the same. God Almighty paved for us a way to pursue Him as our own. Leading people to the knowledge of who Jesus is grants us the understanding God alone builds our way to heaven. If you never apply the ritual of strength that God is your provider, you live without purpose. God has designed our hearts to share Him in a personal manner, and by doing this action, we reaffirm the power of our Lord and Savior. Scripture builds our hearts and develops our minds to understand God is the reason for our existence. Without this understanding, we lose our reflective support, clouding our path. Teach the truth of the Lord thy God and revel in the addiction of purity that springs forward. You will learn support and dive into the depth of trust, where you will feast with pleasure and gain respect. God supports the revealing of His nature. He is our security blanket. By His person, we learn whom to follow and grow with. God is not secretly kept within us. When we know Him, our hearts rejoice for all of mankind to do the same. We enjoy sharing the love of God, and people around us know we care for His person.

Simple acts of trust develop when our hearts apply faith toward the Lord. This action expresses the purity God holds, and we learn to step forth in favor by the will of God in our life. If you feel led to operate in the manner of true faith, God will bless you in the process. He will feed your spirit with good, moral insight, and you will gain hope while progressing in a forward direction of care. God establishes the heart and directs its action through faith and support to the mind. God alone is the caregiver who never fails. By His person, we gain true, moral leverage where all we do becomes a part of the good we see for another. Teaching man to know God is a gift to give freely. You can guide many just by being kind and supportive in a time of need or in gentle conversation. God is the support system where all knowledge flows. It is by His person we are directed to offer others hope and love. Only God crafts the spirit to be led with support that builds in grace and love. God binds the mind and guides it to the realization only He can gain one life eternal. If you are feeling low, think on the way God built up Adam when the curse came into view after the serpent enticed him to take from the tree of the knowledge of good and evil. Which in turn brought death.

The Lord God made garments of skin for Adam and his wife and clothed them. Genesis 3:21 NIV

1 Adam lay with his wife Eve, and she became pregnant and gave birth to Cain. She said, "With the help of the Lord I have brought forth a man." Genesis 4:1 NIV

The Lord is the shepherd to man. He builds so that man can gain and support another just as he has gained. This is, by design, how God implements the work of trust and care. God engineers the mind to move in a forward manner that builds with a support unit designed to breed good favor. God's desire is for man to know how to enable himself to learn and to repeat a skill set gained by experience and instructed measures provided by way of teaching. God has implemented the mind to fester as a solid body of good intent. We gain in the way of enlightenment when our heart is tied to a dream or a goal. They manifest within our person and lead us on a path of righteous endeavors. God alone is the great I Am. Only He can bring a way forward that reaches a level of achievement that brings into play a gain for us to be enhanced. When we operate as a child of God, our mind forms a unity, and we learn by the Master's hand. God is good all the time, so following His lead means we will shelter a growth of good intent. If we pursue the Lord, we are better equipped to manage a structure of strength because He is our support measure. God establishes our heart to manifest the goal He supplies our heart with, bringing us into a design element that focuses on true intent, not that of dark formations. Look to the Lord for any building you desire to do. Man has many talents and gifts offered to him because God is faithful to all people. He creates beauty in man and offers him a path of identity leading to true, moral character where man and God bind as one. Leaving the truth of God out of your daily investment only brings a hardened mental division. If you walk in faith and support of the King, you will learn how true commitment looks, and it will be present in all you do. Manifesting a life without the Lord is dark and unsupportive. The nature of man is to be sinful. Only by pursuing the Lord does one find the meaning of good, and the revelation of unity will appear. Taking steps outside of this will bring into play a loss and no life eternal in the heavenly realm. God supports a person when he establishes a connection to Him. A walk with Jesus is bright and supportive. Darkness has no home if God is the one you relate to. Talking to God is simple. A simple prayer can obtain much favor. Look at how Ester brought a change for a nation by praying for her people group to be protected. She understood God loved her alongside that of her heritage line.

15 Then Ester sent this reply to Mordecai: 16 "Go, gather together all the Jews who are in Susa, and fast for me. Do not eat or drink for three days, night or day. I and my maids will fast as you do. When this is done, I will go to the king, even though it is against the law. And if I perish, I perish." 17 So Mordecai went away and carried out all of Esther's instructions. Esther 4:15-17 NIV

5 "If it pleases the king," she said, "and if he regards me with favor and thinks it the right thing to do, and if he is pleased with me, let an order be written overruling the dispatches that Haman son of Hammedatha, the Agagite, devised and wrote to destroy the Jews in all the king's provinces. 6 For how can I bear to see disaster fall on my people? How can I bear to see the destruction of my family?" 7 King Zerxes replied to Queen Esther and to Mordecai the Jew, "Because Haman attacked the Jews, I have given his estate to Esther, and they have hanged him on the gallows. 8 Now write another decree in the king's name on behalf of the Jews as seems best to you, and seal it with the king's signet ring-for no document written in the king's name and sealed with his ring can be revoked." Esther 8:5-8 NIV

11 The king's edict granted the Jews in every city the right to assemble and protect themselves; to destroy, kill, and annihilate any armed force of any nationality or province that might attack them and their women and children; and to plunder the property of their enemies. Esther 8:11 NIV

God offers man the understanding that He alone is the caregiver of support. By the power of God, man is enlightened. His heritage is understood, and man gleans knowledge about the true character of the Most High. God is offering you a better format for healing. Look to the table of love and dine on the hope God provides. He can perform a miracle within your person. By His hand, you can obtain a clear slate of purity. God offers the slice of heaven known as the gift of gain, which computes to a release of favor through faith and hope. The Father builds a lasting mental perspective, and once this is realized, gain is achieved. God is a builder where man and He are one—tied as a bouquet of love where the heart and mind find freedom. The pain one feels from a divorce or loss of a partner due to marital discord leaves the heart in disarray. Healing is achieved when God becomes the focus of the heart instead of the injury and its constraints. When God manifests as a genuine partner, you are enhanced in the understudy of real unity.

When the application of trust is adhered to, much gain is presented. God the Father is ever faithful, and He will advance your goal set when you work toward the unity He offers. God organizes a plan and manifests an option that breeds life into your heart. God alone can build where man cannot. If you follow in faith and acknowledge the Lord is the giver of all good things, you realize God can move for you in such a manner that you blossom and create good intent alongside the glory of goodwill and hope. God never invades the mind with a dark encounter. His light is always a way forward. By supporting the King, much gain is seen and witnessed. Even in the dark, God can make a way. He can bend the light toward the bounty of faith and produce a beauty of gold. God pursues you with care. He never breaches your heart in a manner of doubt or loss. With God, you can build and support others alongside your own goal. In doing so, one learns the true bond of love created by the Savior. He is forthright and righteous. With God, a bounty is witnessed, and true faith is a mainstay. God reveals the best way forward; it is understood that light is present. God always invests with care. Never does He bring a dark manner. By the power of faith expressed from the heart, man can find true salvation and a gift of unity because God supports him. Alone, man is nothing but a dark cloud. It is due to his sinful nature. We are created to have free will.

It is a gift, but we often fall prey to dark entrapments because of our weak nature. A little gain in the right format builds a light with care.

This is the manner God embellishes upon. In His forthright manner, all of mankind can find faith and support. God loves all of man. He does not distinguish between wealth and famine. He is a supporter of all that is good and right. Because of this truth, we can invest in God and know He will reward us personally for our trust in Him. God supplies our heart and mind with good support no matter our age or situation of finances. This is something that presents as optional to many. The understanding that God loves all of man is an expression of His good, moral righteousness. Our God is ever right and true. In Him, we find peace and support. Our favor in Him breeds a gain that the heart acknowledges when we trust in the good God brings to the table of life. Every investment we make toward the King brings a light to the mind of another. That is the way God offers through our person a way forward for the lost or confused. When God is our greatest guide, we learn the real commitment of governing a body of people even if we only cast a shadow of little covering. God uses our willing steps and makes seeds of them.

A kind word can support many. This is a simple understanding of what God is like to us personally. If you have heard a word of encouragement, know the Lord's hand was guiding the voice that spoke to you. If this seems hard to believe, think about how you felt when God enabled you to hear the gift of words. This is a spiritual gifting as it spoke to you directly, and you recognized care and unity with the person who granted you favor. That person was guided by the hand of God. Remember, God is all good things. Comprehending this is not easy for some, but the person who believes God is in all they do relates to Him as the great I Am. God organizes the heart in many forms. He builds a clear revelation when the timing is in the correct order. He does not operate without a purpose.

Taking time to build with care supports the good of man. Through the bounty, it represents one can bind a soul to the person of Jesus and bring a life toward the cross with clear unity and support. How we do this is, by following the teaching of God, sharing His instruction of the Bible and knowing God works the rest of the details to His glory. If ever you are in doubt, think about the people of the Old Testament and how they grew in favor. Some were tellers of the Word of God, and they had goals of sharing scripture to better equip others for the cause of Christ Jesus. You can find an example of this by reading the work of David in the Book of Psalms.

> *Blessed is he who has regard for the weak; the Lord delivers him in times of trouble. 2 The Lord will protect him and preserve his life; he will bless him in the land and not surrender him to the desire of his foes. 3 The Lord will sustain him on his sickbed and restore him from his bed of illness. Psalm 41:1-3 NIV*

God has many ways of bringing a clear unity with His heart. He can organize a get together with someone you may need to hear a word of encouragement from, or perhaps a message of hope will be shared. When hosting a group of people, be courteous and support them as a whole. Give all time and care, being kind with love as a goal. Everyone will bond and grow in the manner of friendship, and as a result, many will remember the event with warm regards. Working in the gifted way of speech is a simple gesture most are able to perform. The kindness offered will spread, and shoots of love will manifest. If one cannot communicate with a pronounced emphasis on leadership, genuine care can be provided simply by having your heart express words of concern. An ailing body is given hope when a person gifts a kind notice to the ailment. Wounds run deep in many forms, from paralysis of the heart to bodily pain. All infect the heart and mind, so giving someone time is a precious way to show good communication and care. Leading a group of people to communicate in a manner of good, moral conduct is a gift in and of itself. Not all people can lead and spend quality endeavors in the manner of authority. Look at what God was able to bring to the life of Mary when she first learned she was to carry the Son of God. She relinquished her manner and followed the lead God put forth. As a result, the Savior of the world was created, and man now has a bridge to God the Father. It was a sacrifice in care and supported the heart of man for all generations.

God works all things for good. It may take time but trust His leadership to be accurate and precise. Doors may open outside of the original goal but know God has a plan. He knows the best way to operate and will proceed when the time is exactly right. He does not make errors, nor will He place you in a situation that would cause hardship to you personally. When the timing is sufficient for you to master a goal, He will provide a way ahead. God is stable in the way He builds. He manifests artwork that is correct and beautifully built. It may be something simple or complex in design, but the support will be made clear in the end. During the process, God will make available a growth where your heart and mind gain truth. He works so man will know Him in a personal way. His objective is for all people to learn unity with His person. God operates as a guide who knows the ins and outs of all adventures. He crafts a clear and direct offering that builds truth and leads one to a bountiful harvest. God will devise a plan, and you will adhere to truth during the process. His stand is always righteous. He never makes fraudulent opportunities. With God, you can surmise a good outcome. He will lead with the fruit of the heart being His main purpose.

God's walk with His people is solid, and it breeds truth. The care offered from the hand of God is sufficient for all who pursue Him. God will not fail anyone who supports Him. If you favor more aid, think about how God built up His people during the trial of the Red Sea parting. This had to have been a miracle in the eyes of man. Today we read about it in the verses below.

21 Then Moses stretched out his hand over the sea, and all that night the Lord drove the sea back with a strong east wind and turned it into dry land. The waters were divided, 22 and the Israelites went through the sea on dry ground, with a wall of water on their right and on their left. Exodus 14:21-22 NIV

God's work in His people is always clear and bright. He will offer you a gift of unity, and through the gifting, you will inhale a triangle of care that supports your heart and understanding. Through the love of God, man can learn how to better find faith, and this will enable the heart to breed favor from the Most High. A love of God will bring into play a graft, and many will claim truth as a result. Influences lead our actions. Whom we pursue will direct our thought processes, so taking action involving love and kindness will bring greater unity than direct confusion, where one advances in the dark realm. God cares about all of mankind. He does not discriminate. If you feel led to operate above sound understanding and choose a dark shadow, your healing will not come about. Your wound will fester, and bleed lies to your heart, and you will not gain in the manner of faith or support from God. God has ordained man to know Him personally, and this is His goal for all people. A light that reflects love is always the way forward. Think about God as the Savior of the world as this is truth. Realize God can move a mountain on your behalf. He is faithful and just, and His goal in your life is good. He alone can build you up and lift your spirit toward the light. Plant your heart in His hand and gain unity that unfolds as solid character and good, moral support.

God is a caretaker and supporter of the art field of love. In Him, you will find respect and support not otherwise available to you. He is the one who designs a field of beauty as your backdrop. In Christ, man gains hope. This is good care. This is the way forward.

Robin (Rochel) Arne

Message Six

God Can Perform as a
Master in All He Does

God is a partner to mankind, and He never deviates to the dark side. Man can find hope, supportive goals, and unity in His person. God supplies a moral unity where His heart is tied to man's. A person's future goals should relate to the power God holds in their life. If you are driving toward the union of perfect clarity, look to the Savior for this gift. He is faithful and will breed into you a doorway where you will see clearly. God supports man when the desire is for others to know Him personally. We are all designed to share God with all we meet. If you have this desire, you have obtained the union God put forth in your heart. If you build with the clear motive of guiding another to the love of God, you have gained wisdom. All of man is subject to the day of judgment. Not knowing the Most High personally is a loss that builds darkness in the heart. No one will rejoice in hell. It is torment and anguish that is unbearable. Many are deceived into thinking it will simply be a place where God is not present. What they don't understand is God is light. If God is not there, total darkness will be in His place. There will be no good thing as God is goodness. God will operate with care for those who pursue Him and those who believe in Him. This takes action. Reading the Bible is what shows one the way to think and operate. Without this guidance, how does one know where to go or how to behave? It is also what binds man to God in the way of a personal relationship with Him. Don't fall into the trap of thinking you can live life day by day with no ownership in who the King is to you personally. You learn who God is by investing in His Word, the Bible. Yes, people on their deathbeds have found salvation; this is by the grace of God. No one person can say God did not reveal Himself to him in one form or another, but the clarity of who God is comes from reading scripture. Walking in the way of truth comes with the guidance of God. If one applies his heart to the knowledge contained in the Bible, he is better equipped to support God in a righteous manner. Leaving the Word of the Lord out of your life does not show support for the King. It does not breed wellness of life or capture God's attention to you personally. Knowing God is an investment well worth your time and energy. Look at how David worked with God during his trial against Saul in the cave of darkness. God kept David safe and secure when Saul sought to destroy him.

8 Then David went out of the cave and called out to Saul, "My lord the king!" When Saul looked behind him, David bowed down and prostrated himself with his face to the ground. 9 He said to Saul, "Why do you listen when men say, 'David is bent on harming you'? 10 This day you have seen with your own eyes how the Lord delivered you into my hands in the cave. Some urged me to kill you, but I spared you; I said, 'I will not lift my hand against my master, because he is the Lord's anointed.' 11 See, my father, look at this piece of your robe in my hand! I cut off the corner of your robe but did not kill you. Now understand and recognize that I am not guilty of wrongdoing or rebellion. I have not wronged you, but you are hunting me down to take my life. 12 May the Lord judge between you and me. And may the Lord avenge the wrongs you have done to me, but my hand will not touch you. 13 As the old saying goes, 'From evildoers come evil deeds,' so my hand will not touch you. 1 Samuel 24:8-13 NIV

The supplier of truth is King Jesus. His way of presenting life will always support that of love. He is a caregiver and a person of great understanding. The work He offers to a man's heart will grant peace, and a bond of love will form. Jesus performs in a righteous manner. His skill set is genuine and supports the Father at all times. The two are tied as one. Never doubt God offers a plan of unity to build you up in nature and giftedness. He can make a pauper a wealthy man in a moment or create a life of good, moral conduct and release a spirit of true intent. God supports you always, so believe in Him as a caretaker.

God can build a formation that rights a wrong that was bestowed upon you. In this way, you can gain aid to heal and carry another in the same manner. God does not slight a person for his shortcomings. He enables growth to administer the needed course of action and, by doing so, develops the heart simultaneously.

God the Father builds much for man. He crafts with skill and operates in the realm of unity for all mankind. The light of God's hand on your heart is solid, and it brings unity to the goal of grace and support. When you further the gain of another individual much reward comes your way. God cares about all of man. He invests in the people who put energy in the unity of care. If you follow the lead of the Most High, you learn where to tread and how to operate to bring light and guidance to many. God bears the responsibility of being the lead, and with His support, you will know good measure. The love of God builds when you follow His directive. A walk with the person of the Most High grants the union of care that all of man needs to survive. Look at who God entrusted with the love He brought in the scripture of Romans. Paul supported God and worked as a caregiver to man's heart.

> ***1 Paul, a servant of Christ Jesus, called to be an apostle and set apart for the gospel of God- 2 the gospel he promised beforehand through his prophets in the Holy Scriptures 3 regarding his Son, who as to his human nature was a descendant of David, 4 and who through the Spirit of holiness was declared with power to be the Son of God by his resurrection from the dead: Jesus Christ our Lord. 5 Through him and for his name's sake, we received grace and apostleship to call people from among all the Gentiles to the obedience that comes from faith. 6 And you also are among those who are called to belong to Jesus Christ. Romans 1:1-6 NIV***

God is at work in all of man. He supports the goal of building and creating for the love of one another. If you operate in good faith, things of importance will come your way. You will be gifted with a union where God grants knowledge and a secure way forward. He manifests in the person who looks to Him for their lead. God is available to all of mankind. Through His leadership, a blessed bounty unfolds. Yes, some achieve wealth and do not support the Savior, but their riches will burn away on judgment day. If your goal is to supply your family and friends with hope you are on the right track to salvation. God is the lead and maker of unity where light and favor meet together in a cloud of grace and support.

If salvation is a purpose you desire, accepting the love of God must be what you set your heart upon. God needs to be the reason you exist. Your goals need to align with Him, and your heart needs to invest in His person. This takes place when the mind engages in the truth that God is a support mechanism. God is always available to relate with. He is purposeful, and He builds goals of light. He does not step into the realm of negative caves, as He alone is all good. The Lord is a person of greatness. Through Him alone, one finds life eternal. Jesus sacrificed His life so man could meet His Father and be as one with Him as He (Christ) is. Jesus is God and man in one. He is all man and all God. How this is possible is by the hand of God. He alone could craft something so detailed and glorious. We are small compared to God, yet He still cares for our every need. The smallest detail does not escape His knowledge. God manifests our hearts, and we learn how to present as He does. Our nature and our being become like Him in that we achieve the goal of building one another up. If you enjoy knitting and share your skill set, this is an example of how God works in you to help others reach their own crafting achievement. Sharing your heart's desires can set in motion a bounty that represents a goal of intertwined good conduct for both you and the receiver of your gifting.

The look of love God presents is no secret, nor is it hidden away. God cares and supports us so we may better know His character. Think about how God has gifted you in the way of talent and know He alone gave you the ability to operate in such a manner. He rewards man with love, which develops and thrives in an environment of truth. If you find you care for many, this is something the Lord has gifted you with. He enjoys seeing His children work with one another. It moves Him to a place of greatness. God is special in that He alone can care for all of man. He does this in many forms. Recognizing the lead of God brings light to this understanding. If you occupy a graft of manners that builds to the heart of man, know God is at the helm of your goals. God designs all of His people to love and grow one another.

God is known by His people. Those who serve Him are tied to His way of being. No one person works alone. We all need others to build upon our hearts. If divorce has torn you limb from limb, healing can ensue by relating to the love you hold and connecting it to the King. If you focus on Jesus in place of the one who injured your heart, you will mature and gain hope. God can build you up and restore your way of thinking to a level of great gain. With God, man finds a gateway where the heart and the mind believe in good support. God does not manufacture doubt about His goal setting nor deny a mind the bounty of grace. God knows the injury runs deep, and He is considerate of the wound. He will bind your mind and give it an avenue of love to surround itself with truth and care. God does not leave anyone in the rearview mirror. He never steps away, nor does He lead you in the dark. If you find you are torn in two and have lost the hope you once contained within, let God be the resource you lean into. God will make a way for your heart to be renewed so that growth occurs. He leads in unity so you will hear and understand how He operates, and it will be refreshing to your spirit. With God, hope arrives freely with no strings attached. He is a caregiver of concern and forthright manners.

God is a supporter where all He offers is right and true. It is hard to imagine as man is simple minded, but God is genuine. He never lies or cheats a person. Through the spirit of God, man finds the peace that builds and completes his mind and heart. Only God can build in such a manner. Through His support, a person gains a reprieve so healing can ensue. Look at who brought life to you when you were born. God is a creator. He enjoys building and bringing life to people. His desire is for you to know Him as a solid investor who will never leave your side. This is positive truth, and it supports the character of the Most High. Read where Jesus laid His hand upon the leper and brought healing to him out of love.

13 Naaman's servants went to him and said, "My father, if the prophet had told you to do some great thing, would you not have done it? How much more, then, when he tells you, 'Wash and be cleansed'!" 14 So he went down and dipped himself in the Jordan seven times, as the man of God had told him, and his flesh was restored and became clean like that of a young boy. 15 Then Naaman and all his attendants went back to the man of God. He

stood before him and said, "Now I know that there is no God in all the world except in Israel. Please accept now a gift from your servant." 2 Kings 5:13-15 NIV

The Lord worked for Naaman by way of a prophet, but He was the one with the power. It was by God's hand the healing took place. God often works through others for our gain. A word of wisdom may befall your heart, and understanding may come to you where you unite for the truth to others. God can build in a manner where others learn from your experiences. This brings to light a treasure of information where hope can abound because faithfulness was put forth. If you find it hard to believe God would shower you with care and support, remember you are His child whom He loves and serves. The moment of decision making comes with a call to the spirit. God will work in you and bring to your heart the unity He desires for you to gain. He never separates the mind in such a manner that you are not in control. He simply impresses to your heart His lead. Pursuing His directive will enhance you and set you free from pain. Stepping in unity with God brings a clear path forward. God delivers on His promises, and they are good. Reading the Bible will enhance your goal decision making, and you will feel gain come forth.

The balance of trust presents to you a leadership where you and God act as one. He will lead you in the direct path of fortitude, and you will be at peace. Healing is a gain even though to man, it may appear as a stranglehold. That is because man desires revenge when the pain of injury has been inflicted to the region of love surrounding the heart. We prefer to see the person who injured us suffer, but this is not how one learns to love and favor. God is purposeful in all His ways. A way of thinking must be present in the manner of gifted hope. The goal must be for truth to enlighten the entire thought process. This, in turn, will grant the knowledge that God is superior to our own thinking and justification. Man holds a grudge and feeds it with lies unless God delivers insight on how to perceive the situation. We often lose footing when a divorce takes claim to our life. With God, forward growth can bring to light the proper way to think, and healing then takes form.

The Lord is the giver of faith, which is needed to produce love and honest integrity. God's hand never overreaches, but it does encapsulate the heart and bring it to a growth in care. Loving a person means a risk is involved. No one has a guarantee concerning a commitment when a marriage takes place. Vows are written to remind a person he has made a claim to another in faith, but many lose face and fall short of the bond they committed to. This is not a reflection of the value of a person. It is simply an act of the enemy of God attacking His people and causing loss and destruction. Satan revels in the divorce scene. It causes families to split and children to suffer. Even the party who instigated the divorce loses. It may not be relevant to him in the beginning, but over time truth presents itself, and guilt transpires. Satan will heap the lie of divorce on anyone looking to another for comfort outside the marriage bed.

Adultery is a major cause for the division of a union between a man and wife. God can restore the heart and make it centered with Him as the lead. Gain will again come into view, and healing will transpire. Today many find solace in the arms of lies. God does not inhibit the heart in the event a lie is preferred. However, God has the best insight into what should stand and be embraced. You learn the truth by following His standards. Satan brings the look of great hope when he entices the mind, but in reality, it is death on a platter that glistens with enticement. The way ahead is always found in the Word of the Lord. Standing as a warrior in faith will build good character. Your family will witness someone who loves truth and adheres to the body of life.

Teach the children in the way they should go, and favor will be upon them. Divorce can bring division within the family unit. Jealousy sets in, and disrespect takes over in many forms. A child can see through the facade of an affair. It is present in the way one delivers their voice or actions. It is not hidden though many believe they are smarter than God. He states all sin will be revealed at some point or another. It is not wise counsel if you feel led to deceive your spouse. Your body will decay in a way you don't understand, and you will invite the devil into your intimate self. Decay is a part of life, but it will be enhanced in the event you offer your precious self toward the lean of Satan. A little deception leads to the belief you will never be caught, but know that a counterpart usually suspects and hurts just the same. The goal of unity should start at the throne of the Most High. By His example, we learn the commitment of a true saint. God's power is genuine, and He is able to relieve us of the burden of self-denial. The way God operates is holy and right. He never invents deceptive goals or partners in a manner of lying behavior. God alone never sins, but you will find His grace is sufficient for you. Falling into the trap of hate often brings forth a goal of division where God cannot operate. He won't lead you toward the throne if you conspire against another out of a sheer longing to destroy. Deceptive plans breed danger, so avoid this form of action so you gain an upright lead of strength.

God has a promise for His people. He will always guide and support us even when the darkness is underway. He will place a shield around you, and you will be secure with a fortune of gold and silver. This means His shelter is precious and saving in the manner of unity, good, moral righteousness. If you find a loophole is present and you think God won't notice a slight invested dark crusade where your heart is attached to sin in a negative manner, you are mistaken. He knows all of our desires. A message of truth gives light to the dark. Taking it to heart is what will guide your thought process. If salvation is needed, God will deliver into the offering of the Lamb, His Son, and you will share in the life eternal. Walking in the way of light brings to the heart and mind a path where all you desire becomes tied to the King. People learn God has the better path where faith and hope blossom and grow, partnered in unity toward the goal of a beautiful future.

Temptation builds the more it is fed. It is deceptive as it will never be complete. It will only lead you to a path of loss. The decision to gain in the goal of a partnership with Jesus brings forth a beauty where all purpose and intent are tied to the Master's hand. God will protect you from harm, and He will aid your brokenness in the event a loss has occurred. It is God's way to invest and give an opportunity to those in need of His care. Even if you are suffering due to false pretenses and have learned you will no longer be partnered with your mate, God can bring truth, and you can gain freedom in love. God is all powerful, and He delivers the truth to those who pursue Him. God will always gift one with His person. Simply ask the Lord to speak to you in a personal manner. He will reveal to you His heart, and you will gain instruction to better equip your heart and mind to stand in the time of trial. Shouldering the burden alone will not bring about healing. Only God can create the salve that releases the mind into focus where love can abide. God gifts the heart with good care and limits the doubt, so you learn the truth and how to keep it secure within your person. A trail of pain from relationships that blew apart is often a result of divorce, as no healing and growth have been acquired. Testing the limits of God's timing is not a goal to adhere to. Let the Lord lead and prescribe how you are to step. You will find it secure and forthright, and you will gain unity at the same time. God offers the value of man to the recognition He is a caregiver.

God's perspective is separate from man's. His goal of unity requires a person to step in faith and support the content God delivers. All God's gifts are righteous and good, so there is no better way to move ahead than by following the Lord's guided commandments. They represent hope and a way ahead. They are clear with purpose and support all the Lord's desires for man. A shoulder of respect is secure when it divulges the unity displayed at the cross. Believing God can build and support you starts the motion of good intent. It is amazing the truth that is shared when a person invests in reading scripture. Even a verse or two can bring enlightenment. Starting the discovery process can be burdensome to the mind when it is a simple maneuver. The time you share with God will support your heart in the manner of great return. God's disciples understood this gesture and wrote with care all the encompassing words of scripture. Many were prophets, and some were even laymen. God has a purpose for everyone. Scripture is purposeful, and it breeds love on every page. The contents are honest, and a union is gained. It is by God's design that man can relate to His person. He gifted this unity on the page of Psalm 40:4-5.

4 Blessed is the man who makes the Lord his trust, who does not look to the proud, to those who turn aside to false gods. 5 Many, O Lord my God, are the wonders you have done. The things you planned for us no one can recount to you; were I to speak and tell of them, they would be too many to declare. Psalm 40:4-5 NIV

God will contain the pain, and He will supply a reprieve. He is bountiful and resourceful. His care supports the goal of gain, so you are set free from loss or harm in Him. It may seem unrighteous to praise during a heartbreak, but this draws the Lord close to you. Opening your mind to the care He offers brings light and solid unity in His direction. God leads and maneuvers the goal of unity in all situations. Only we have control over whether we allow Him to lead our life. God will not push His way into your goal set. However, He will enhance your unity in the placement of true righteousness. If you choose outside of God's way, you will remain seething, and the injury you suffer will not heal. God's way is prosperous and true. It is a solid endeavor, and you will grow in peace when you bend to the will of God. His alignment will aid you spiritually, and you will be vastly numbered as righteous when you follow the plan of God. Sin is in the nature of man, so attending to the direct root cause is where you need to operate from. God seeds the mind with solid gain where man enjoys his own understanding. If you choose wisdom and gain over loss and failure, you will lean into God's arms and grow in care and support. A wise gesture of faith leads one to a clear step in the right direction. God always makes way for the loss to be washed by the wayside. Yes, the memory will remain, but the crippling injury will no longer contain your mind. You will grow in support, and the truth of God will be revealed. If you are the one who invested and had your way of life destroyed by another, you are more likely to harbor a grudge. This is the case for anyone who committed in faith and expected the same in return. God knows your loss and understands the connection you had and how it has been severed. But He alone has the antidote where you can become healed and restored to good gain once more. The beauty a heart contains can lose its luster if bitterness stays in the realm of the thought process. Goal setting of better thoughts happens when God is the focus of the heart.

God leads and supports in the manner of righteous goal setting. He never leaves the injury unattended, and He breathes a new line of favor toward the gain a person needs. If you have lost the major counterpart in your life, you have been left with a gaping hole within your person. Fill it with the love God offers freely and securely. The shining manner of unity God provides fills the open wound and shelters it with care. The witness God has given to our hearts leads with the knowledge He is caring and supportive in the way He operates. God delivers on His promises, and this is understood in the Book of Romans.

1 Therefore, since we have been justified through faith, we have peace with God through our Lord Jesus Christ, 2 through whom we have gained access by faith into this grace in which we now stand. And we rejoice in the hope of the glory of God. 3 Not only so, but we also rejoice in our sufferings, because we know that suffering produces perseverance; 4 perseverance, character; and character, hope. 5 And hope does not disappoint us, because God has poured out his love into our hearts by the Holy Spirit, whom he has given us. Romans 5:1-5 NIV

God is always connected to the people who engage with His person. He supports them and leads them with good care. God is a machine of integrity. All He offers man is gauged with good, moral righteousness. God cannot sin. It is not in His nature, so this is a guarantee you will never be injured by Him. Unity is the heart of His directive. God will correct and chastise when sin is present, but He will not forget His love of man. He never fades away. He is always available and ready to bend an ear to your cry. Your concern never leaves His boundary of understanding, and He stands erect to your person. God lifts the heart of man in a manner that leads to good intent. Trials come and go, but with God as the operative in your life, they will not consume you. Many find solace in the arms of the flesh. This is deception, and it won't bring gain. Sex is an influence that leads to doubt because no man or woman can heal a pain or make it right and true. Sex leads many into the deceptive behavior of foolish walking. It feeds on the material of lust alone, so it has no substance of goodness. Marriage brings the covenant of life, so the relationship of two people in the manner is life-giving. However, today many feel marriage is not important, and they believe they can live in sin and be free from consequences. This deception breeds a loss of unity from the Most High to the unity of two people trying to live as one. Marriage is a covenant that supports the truth God is a union maker. Church messages bring light to this teaching, but many fall short concerning the scripture to support the unity described above. Look at how David fell when he slept with a married woman. As a result, he lost a son and suffered the pain of fault. God restored him, but the injury remained in his mind.

13 Then David said to Nathan, "I have sinned against the Lord." Nathan replied, "The Lord has taken away your sin. You are not going to die. 14 But because by doing this you have made the enemies of the Lord show utter contempt, the son born to you will die." 15 After Nathan had gone home, the Lord struck the child that Uriah's wife had borne to David, and he became ill. 16 David pleaded with God for the child. He fasted and went into his house and spent the nights lying on the ground. 17 The elders of his household stood beside him to get him up from the ground, but he refused, and he would not eat any food with them. 18 On the seventh day the child died. David's servants were afraid to tell him that the child was dead, for they thought, "While the child was still living, we spoke to David, but he would not listen to us. How can we tell him the child is dead? He may do something desperate." 19 David noticed that his servants were whispering among themselves, and he realized the child was dead. "Is the child dead?" he asked. "Yes, they replied, "he is dead." 2 Samuel 12:13-19 NIV

The mark of a man is not how much his bank account holds but who he supports and leads in the knowledge God is supportive and good. Anyone who believes in the Father and His Son has gained life eternal with purpose and faith. The light of God is ever more, and through this gain, man understands the hope God has made available. Never think God won't act on your behalf when pain is in the arena of your life. God favors the mind that leads another to the knowledge God is a caretaker. If you lead another to the goal of a bountiful harvest in the manner of unity, God will see your good form, and a blessing will ensue. How God brings this gift is known only to Him. It may not look like what you would expect, but it will be good. God knows our nature, and He gifts us in the manner of great support, which in turn will prosper our own goal setting. If you lead and believe God is all-powerful and have the unity God has supplied within your heart, then it has taken root. God knows how best to be supportive, for our nature may require restraint in the department of financial influence, or there may be a better support measure God leans our way. If you find favor in leading others, remember God has placed you there to support, not tear down. Leading has responsibility; one day, you will have to offer the knowledge of what you were supporting when judgment comes. God knows the heart, and He embraces a willing gift of unity toward the goal of care. God, the Father, is always supportive in all He does. None can compare to the way God builds or structures the mind.

People in the market square of doubt often develop a fear where no love will be rewarded. Feeling as though no one cares brings a loss that the heart can't endure. Look at family and believe God has them in your life for a reason. Lean on their goals of good form and support the idea you are important to them. We often neglect to realize our parents are usually always in our court of alliance. If we have siblings, they too, will come to bat for us when we feel alone. Growing in the unity of family is a worthwhile way to live. Our family unit supports us when we are in pain. They can be more objective when we are in need of guidance, and their insight can lead us to a better perspective. Often, a person will fall victim to a loss in one form or another. Our lives will always be impacted in some manner that expresses we lived and had important ideas. If we build with care, our hearts will expand and invite good, relational grounds that create unity and sound, moral leadership. God brings us to His person when pain has transpired. He draws our hearts to Him through the love of His Son, Jesus. When a person looks to God for instruction, good, righteous ways evolve. The witness one portrays is what sets him apart from the crowd.

We can offer others good conduct or hide the truth we learn and fail in the ministry of love found by reading the Word of God. Each story in the Bible holds a value that is pure and forthright. All the words express love from the Most High. He has grafted us to Him in the manner of lengthy expression. The reading needs to contain verses geared to the heart, which all of them do. If you look at the scripture tied to Rebekah, you will find a value of strength where she planted her heart with a man God brought by way of distinct manner and care. They were bonded by care and given a ministry of guidance that showered their hearts and minds with a glow of purity.

59 So they sent their sister Rebekah on her way, along with her nurse and Abraham's servant and his men. 60 And they blessed Rebekah and said to her, "Our sister, may you increase to thousands upon thousands; may your offspring possess the gates of their enemies." 61 then Rebekah and her maids got ready and mounted their camels and went back with the man. So the servant took Rebekah and left. 62 Now Isaac had come from Beer Lahai Roi, for he was living in the Negev. 63 He went out to the field one evening to meditate, and as he looked up, he saw camels approaching. 64 Rebekah also looked up and saw Isaac. She got down from her camel 65 and asked the servant, "Who is that man in the field coming to meet us?" "He is my master," the servant answered. So she took her veil and covered herself. 66 Then the servant told Isaace all he had done. 67 Isaac brought her into the tent of his mother Sarah, and he married Rebekah. So she became his wife, and he loved her; and Isaac was comforted after his mother's death. Genesis 24:59-67 NIV

The heart of man is ever faithful when God is the one being the standard of measure. God brings clarity to the mind and offers gain where all we learn and prosper from is tied to His good name. Even the person who professes there is no God has been gifted, and he simply does not recognize it was God at work in His life. God is limitless. Through His power, we gain love and fruit of the heart. The time of unity is always at hand. Binding your thought process to God will deliver your standard, and you will build strength where all you think upon is good and morally just. Looking to the Savior builds equity that maintains our goal set. God, the Father, is a faithful being. He does not step aside when we slip or fall in our walk with Him. He stands at the ready to always lead and guide us in a forthright manner. His integrity is boundless, so you never have to worry about Him leading you astray. God is glorious and true. He is beautiful in all he does. He knows how to build with character and strength, and He supports the heart of man in total righteousness. His manner of integrity always gains our hearts a way forward. The shadow a man invests in will darken if God does not offer His helping hand. We all need guidance, and with God, we find all the needed knowledge in His Book of light. The Bible contains the written manner of good intent. With every phrase and verse, we are guided with care.

God has unity in the way He portrays His Son on the cross of life. It was not misguided in any form. It transpired so man would be able to reside with the Most High, King Jesus. God's love poured forth that day and will forever stand as holy and true. The King could have stepped down and said no, but He loves mankind passionately. Jesus is our Waymaker. Through His discipleship to our heart, we are offered unity with God the Father, our creator, the great I Am. Look at the way God portrays His love in the verses concerning the sacrifice and testimony of support.

16 For God so loved the world that he gave his one and only Son, that whoever believes in him shall not perish but have eternal life. 17 For God did not send his Son into the world to condemn the world, but to save the world through him. John 3:16-17 NIV

The light of the cross is ever before our heart and mind. No one can claim God did not reveal the truth to them at some point in their life. God always builds with hope, whereas the enemy of the Lord tears down and strikes with fear. If you struggle to know what step to take next, trust the Lord to guide you. He is ever faithful, and unity is what He strives to impress upon you. Look at how God builds and think about the course of action that is available. Is it honoring in value? Does it relate to good or deception? If darkness is present, walk on and build in a new formation.

God will provide the light of where to proceed. Often man desires something that glitters with desire, but in reality, it is sin abounding. If you feel led to walk in the light, follow scripture and learn how God operates. The guidance of the King is always the way forward. You will find favor and support, and the lead of God will manifest unity. There will be strength within your person, and the ground will be solid. God's gift to man was light and forthright. It stands as the standard of hope. It is proof God has unity at the core of His being. Being tied to God will shatter the length of pain that has been inflicted, and it will be released from your person.

God cares and will heal your heart if you allow Him to. Looking at the standard God built upon is a clear unity in its design. God offered His greatest gift to us, and we, in turn, need only confess our heart and claim the gift of unity. By expressing Jesus is the way, the truth, and the life, we acknowledge He is who He claims to be. His lead is solid, and it is manifesting in nature. The light of God always desires good for our lives. God contains all of mankind in the manner of provision and support. Even someone on their deathbed can find peace in the arms of God. God supports the love of one to another. He hears our prayers, and when we lift up another, He supports our goal of care. If you find your heart is hurting, begin to form a plan of serving others in prayer. It will open a pathway, and your desire for unity will unfold with great strength. God offers our hearts the ability to further the union with Him and thus bring into the light our path where we can recognize the truth of our circumstances. God lights our minds with truth when we apply the Word of His Bible to our daily life. Knowing God is the one to orchestrate a good way of life gives to our hearts the unity we need to believe and invest in another person. The shower of love grants our minds and gifts us with knowledge.

He alone is the Waymaker where we can develop truth in our hearts and build in good, moral conduct. If we believe God will support our growth when we build in unity with Him, we learn He is all powerful. God expresses His love in many forms. He entertains our minds and instructs them to build unity that supports the good of all. If you feel led to shine as a leader, reading the Word of God will enhance your gain, and you will invest in truth, thus making a clear path ahead. Many find favor is the result of pursuing the great I Am. God is never far from our hearts. He alone is the one to gift love and unity. He is the builder of all things material and the spiritual growth of the heart and mind. You are mistaken if you think you have gained materially all by the labor of your work. God is the one who brought the bounty. By His hand, you were able to create or transpire a good gain. God always leads, even when we can't see the path He has us on. In the dark is where the enemy resides. His goal is to tear down all you build and invest in. Therefore, pursue God and build with His protection. A storm may come and, in its wake, take all of your possessions. This does not mean God is not in control. God allows losses, but He is not one to inflict hardship if you act with purity. Satan creates havoc in many forms but know God is more powerful. With the person of the Lord, there is security which leads to eternal life and hope. Outside of God, there is only death and negative guidance. The Father is kind and supportive, whereas Satan destroys a person even if it appears gain is transpiring. The deceptive nature of God's enemy is not always seen with the naked eye. He can manifest as light, so we need prayer coverage and unity with the Most High. The shadow of God is ever a safety net, whereas the enemy is a destroyer of the heart and mind. God can bring truth to anyone who desires it, but unity with Him must exist. A call to the person of God is forthright and supports the love of God in your own being. Look at where the Savior has planted His manner in the Book of Mark.

46 Then they came to Jericho. As Jesus and his disciples, together with a large crowd, were leaving the city, a blind man, Bartimaeus (that is, the Son of Timaeus), was sitting by the roadside begging. 47 When he heard that it was Jesus of Nazareth, he began to shout, "Jesus, Son of David, have mercy on me!" 48 Many rebuked him and told him to be quiet, but he shouted all the more, "Son of David, have mercy on me!" 49 Jesus stopped and said, "Call him." So, they called the blind man, "cheer up! On your feet! He's calling you." 50Throwing his cloak aside, he jumped to his feet and came to Jesus. 51 "What do you want me to do for you?" Jesus asked him. The blind man said, "Rabbi, I want to see." 52 "Go," said Jesus, "your faith has healed you." Immediately he received his sight and followed Jesus along the road. Mark 10:46-52 NIV

Robin (Rochel) Arne

Message Seven

God Will Lead with Clear Faith and Restore the Mind in Care and Support

The face of God is a beautiful way of life. In Him, one rests with care, and there is a gifted manner of support. Our God never leaves one in the dark. He will light the way ahead and unity will lead with directive attributes. Look at Sarah and observe the gift of love God showed her by standing with her when she desired a child in the face of heartache. God restored her womb, and life was granted in her elder years. This was a miracle of the Lord. He is faithful, even in the latter part of life. He can grant a dream and bring it to life.

> *1 Now the Lord was gracious to Sarah as he had said, and the Lord did for Sarah what he had promised. 2 Sarah became pregnant and bore a son to Abraham in his old age, at the very time God had promised him. 3 Abraham gave the name Isaac to the son Sarah bore him. 4 When his son Isaac was eight days old, Abraham circumcised him, as God commanded him. 5 Abraham was a hundred years old when his son Isaac was born to him. 6 Sarah said, "God has brought me laughter, and everyone who hears about this will laugh with me." 7 And she added "Who would have said to Abraham that Sarah would nurse children? Yet I have borne him a son in his old age." Genesis 21:1-7 NIV*

God builds with respect. If you find a loss has ensued and your heart bleeds with shame, know your Lord is able to perform redemption within your person. Through the blood of the Lord, you are made well. Knowing this is true is what builds up man. The great I Am is faithful in all He does. By His stance, we can find repair to our injuries, and in the process, we gain insight that God is who He claims to be. God is always right. He never makes a mistake. His Word teaches we are people of His heart.

With this reference, we lean into the knowledge that God is great and can bring a gift of gain to us as He wills. The Lord has shown mercy to many people over time. In fact, all people have the available witness if they believe and trust in the King. Jesus is the Waymaker. He is the bridge where we meet the Father. Father God supports our person in such manner that we never need to look elsewhere for support. There is none greater than He.

Teaching others about who the Lord is brings a gift of love that shows care and hope. God is the region of intent that speaks a great love language. His makeup is right and true. You never have to worry about a misstep if God is your compass. When you pursue Jesus, you will find support and light along the way. There may, at some point, be confusion as how to proceed. This may not impede your walk. Look at scripture to know the resolution, then proceed and trust the Lord is at your side. If there is no clear path before you, rest in the knowledge that God is at work on your behalf. Trust Him to lead you when the time is right because He is the one who knows all angles of any situation.

God is able to multiply your net worth in a manner of great strength. However, that may not be His goal for your life. If you struggle daily with paying your bills, know God is at the helm. Stay committed to the way of God, and a release will come into view, and support will rise up. He promises us aid. This may come unexpectedly, so always stay connected to the person of God. How He brings gain may be separate from your plan, but in the end, all will stand as a witness of love, and you will be blessed through the process. God is the light for any constructive opportunity. In Him is found favor which supports the mindset of unity. The ultimate goal of God is to know you as His own. He desires your person to blend with Him in a manner of good moral standing. The shoulder of God is ever broad. He can do all things good and right, so believe He will sort out your investment and make it thrive. When God is moving, much recognition comes His way. Those who evaluate your witness will lean into the knowledge God has crafted through you. Let Him be the one to claim the glory. If you fall victim to pride, the bounty will fade, and loss will ensue. The tower of Babel was one example where man thought he could conquer God and rule over Him.

1 Now the whole world had one language and a common speech. 2 As men moved eastward, they found a plain in Shinar and settled there. 3 They said to each other, "Come, let's make bricks and bake them thoroughly." They used brick instead of stone, and tar for mortar. 4 Then they said, "Come, let us build ourselves a city, with a tower that reaches to the heavens, so that we may make a name for ourselves and not be scattered over the face of the whole earth." 5 But the Lord came down to see the city and the tower that the men were building. 6 The Lord said, "If as one people speaking the same language, they have begun to do this, then nothing they plan to do will be impossible for them. 7 Come, let us go down and confuse their language so they will not understand each other." 8 So the Lord scattered them from there over all the earth, and they stopped building the city. 9 That is why it was called Babel-because there the Lord confused the language of the whole world. From there the Lord scattered them over the face of the whole earth. Genesis 11:1-9 NIV

God formulates a path ahead and secures the heart and mind to do better. With God, a plan is read and believed. God directs in care, and you recognize His good way. If a barrier is present, look at what may be the cause. Are there missions of good intent? Does the build offer a way to connect with the Holy Spirit? Is there gain for others, or is it a sole proprietorship? With God, people are His desire. In the manner of good intent, we work as a team that leads and instructs for the good of many. If you find you favor being alone, you may not be in the will of the Most High. Yes, people need time to themselves, but building just for the sake of yourself is not how God invests in His people. He enjoys it when we connect with one another and work as a team. Today's influence is that of self. It is a far cry from the good God provides. Through the gift of many, thoughts and ideas spread, and good comes forward. Don't be afraid of losing your own worth. We are all made to produce in a good manner. Anyone working outside of God will fail at some point. If recognition is what you desire, there may be an influence of a dark presence near you. Fame is fleeting, and it can be harmful to our mindset.

God does raise up in the way of lordship but know that if you lead others, much is expected of you. God will operate where His presence is desired and built upon. Growing with a unity of good intent is not something man is accustomed to. It is by the leadership of God that man invests with care for the support of another. Jesus is the Waymaker for all of mankind. In Him is found the love and care all man desires. God is a builder of the heart. He does not tear down a work if it is right and true. God will manufacture growth, and support will be apparent. Through the leadership God portrays, you will find unity and a love of good, moral standing. God's favor supports the growth of man when true bonding is taking place. God desires for all to know Him in a personal manner. If you favor good intent, think about how God brought Adam into the garden of Eden. He did it in such a way that Adam was created solely by His person. No other thing was able to build in such a manner. From dust, Adam was created.

7 the Lord God formed the man from the dust of the ground and breathed into his nostrils the breath of life, and the man became a living being. Genesis 1:7 NIV

God, the Father, is a caregiver who leads with love and genuine interest. God never puts forward a loss or a misguided manner. In Him is purity that none can compare to. God never brings dark gifts. His are always good and meaningful with guidance of just works. If you have a balance of hurt and nothing has aided you in the way of healing. God can bring to you a support measure that speaks purity to your soul.

God, the author of perfection, is always at your side. He is steadfast and supportive with the availability of good, moral rest. In God, favor unfolds with concern for many. Our heart is led in the manner of opportunity, and the process of growing in unity is our desire. All God offers to man is worthwhile and bleeds unity. When God supports our desire, we lean into the knowledge He operates in unity, and the drive of our mind will be to better all of mankind. In the event you need healing, pursue the King. He bled on the cross for you, and this shows His love is beyond measure. All God made is beauty and a life-giving invitation to be at His side. No one thing or individual can obtain unity unless God is their focus. Because of God, we learn how to build and craft with good intent. Our unity with Him builds our minds in the path of righteousness. Follow the love of Christ and support those around you. You will inherit a path that unfolds in union with the Most High. This statement is made in value of the Word of God. Look to any verse in the distinct manner of learning, and you will gain insight. The scripture of the Bible contains unity. Each time you invest in reading the contents, you gain a party of three, the Holy Spirit, God the Father, and Jesus Christ the Son. All three support you as one. They unite to create a trinity. The region of unity described in Daniel guarantees our Father is ever faithful. The lions in the den would have eaten the prey of Daniel had God not shut their mouths in order to show His power. This example is well known to many, but the truth it tells is glorious and right.

> *16 So the king gave the order, and they brought Daniel and threw him into the lion's den. The king said to Daniel, "May your God, whom you serve continually, rescue you!" 17 A stone was brought and placed over the mouth of the den, and the king sealed it with his own signet ring and with the rings of his nobles, so that Daniel's situation might not be changed. 18 Then the king returned to his palace and spent the night without eating and without any entertainment being brought to him. And he could not sleep. 19 At the first light of dawn, the king got up and hurried to the lion's den. 20 When he came near the den, he called to Daniel in an anguished voice, "Daniel, servant of the living God, has your God, whom you serve continually, been able to rescue you from the lions?" 21 Daniel answered, "O king, live forever! 22 My God sent his angel, and he shut the mouths of the lions. They have not hurt me, because I was found innocent in his sight. Nor have I ever done any wrong before you, O king." Daniel 6:16-22 NIV*

When a person is in need, God offers His goal of truth so a gain can be had. God relates to man in a manner of faith. By His person, man is able to relate and interact as a being of love. Believing in the power God holds is significant to the gain one desires to inhabit. If you are led by the thought God is ever at your side, you are equipped to further mankind and support the knowledge God works through you to better the relationship of man to God. God supports anyone who incorporates Him into their life. Men enjoy life when they feel accomplished. When God is at work, you harvest grain in the way of unity and leading of the heart and mind. Anyone who looks to God for his ability to flourish realizes God is a Waymaker and a being of love and support. When God crafts the heart, a beauty comes forward. Others who see your change can attest to the goodness you now support where you have grown with favor.

God, the Father, is always a guidance counselor. In Him, one finds a peace and support that flourishes the heart. All of God is good. He will not push you into an arrangement of darkness. He is an expert at the light and the good, moral way. Taking the Word of God to heart is the first step to building a direct opportunity to know Him in a better way. If you desire to heal and you believe God is the way, start by engaging with His person. This is an easy way to operate. Surrender your thought process to the understanding the King has your best interest at heart. Know God will never lift you to a place of doubt or loss. In God, gain is strived for. The shoulder of God is ever broad.

In Him is gain and a bounty of true integrity. No harm will ever be inflicted by God's hand if you walk in the way of true support. God understands mistakes. He will correct your course if you misjudge a way ahead. He is not harsh or repulsed by our inaptness. God, the author of our being, knows us inside and out. Don't feel you aren't good enough for the King Jesus, as He loves all people, great and small. The goal of God is for man to unite with Him personally, creating a union of good love. God is always right with concern. He lives to feed us good intent. You can savor the life of a legend in that Jesus is the one who made your goal setting good. If you have a dream that supports many, look to the Savior to bring it into view. It may take some work, and there may be a wait, but trust God to build good character and unity. The time of investment you make available will breed a union, and life will be had. All the support you can muster will never compare to the God of all man. With God leading the way, your build will have legs. Look at how God built in union with David concerning the temple he desired to craft. God chose another to be the one to do the actual crafting, but David was the one who aided in the containment of wares made available. David was stained with the blood of war, along with the murder of Uriah. God still enabled David to dream and to operate with care and a drive that brought forth hope and good standing.

11 " 'The Lord declares to you that the Lord himself will establish a house for you: 12 When your days are over and you rest with your fathers, I will raise up your offspring to succeed you, who will come from your own body, and I will establish his kingdom. 13 He is the one who will build a house for my Name, and I will establish the throne of his kingdom forever. 2 Samuel 7:11-13 NIV

3 "you know that because of the wars waged against my father David from all sides, he could not build a temple for the Name of the Lord his God until the Lord put his enemies under his feet. 4 But now the Lord my God has given me rest on every side, and there is no adversary or disaster. 5 I intend, therefore, to build a temple for the Name of the Lord my God, as the Lord told my father David, when he said, 'Your son whom I will put on the throne in your place will build the temple for my Name.' 1 Kings 5:3-5 NIV

51 When all the work King Solomon had done for the temple of the Lord was finished, he brought in the things his father David had dedicated-the silver and gold and furnishings-and he placed them in the treasuries of the Lord's temple. 1 Kings 7:51 NIV

When a body is in ailment, a pain ensues where help is needed in some form or another. God has the salve to strengthen and heal in ways no representative of another care can support. Only God can bring to the forefront a remedy where heart and mind act as one. With God, support is fast and solid. All God offers is righteous and good. Never doubt God can move a mountain in healing for you when you trust His superior being to aid you in a manner of love and faith. God, the Father, is a caregiver where hope and love possess the skill set of restoration to the mind. Once that transpires, the heart soon follows. The love of the Most High is just. It does not kill or destroy in any form. God supplies man with the gift of unity; in doing so, the balance of care unfolds.

Many find they have a fear of the Lord. They believe Him to be harsh or mean in some manner. God desires for man to live a life of union that supports gain. If you pursue the Lord, honest goals will assimilate. When the Lord gifts the mind with His way of being, a knowledge of faith ensues. God, the Father, can manifest and portray a way ahead where all you pursue is righteous and good. There is always gain to be had when you trust the Lord with your goal setting. Each step you take toward the person of God delivers a value of true intent. Following in the manner of trust is a way to know the King and His truth. Read below how God orchestrated the lead for Micah to be able to bend to the will of the true leader. In Him was made a great honor for many to learn the truth.

6 "In that day," declares the Lord, "I will gather the lame; I will assemble the exiles and those I have brought to grief. 7 I will make the lame a remnant, those driven away a strong nation. The Lord will rule over them in Mount Zion from that day and forever. 8 As for you, O watchtower of the flock, O stronghold of the Daughter of Zion, the former dominion will be restored to you; kingship will come to the Daughter of Jerusalem." Micah 4:6-8 NIV

Favor from God builds us in a manner of great hope. By pursuing God's love, we learn where true honor and respect originate. The lead God offers is right, and it builds in the way of true, noble mentorship. God, the Father, is a caregiver. He creates a love that is endless in its design. When we allow God the authority to move within our person, we gain in value to His person. God is forthright and pure. In Him is all good and righteous manners. The lead of God is always a statement of unity. If you feel led to seek more gain, look to Christ for advancement. He paves the way for more truth, thus producing a unity that builds and constructs with care. The goal of the Father is for us to better know His person. When we read the Word of the Lord, our presence gains unity, and good intent ensues. We become a being of strength, and hope follows thereafter. Our guardianship is that of the Father Himself, so we are protected and well cared for, all the while being made in the image of God. If you value strength and good unity, God is the one to pursue. A life of existence leads to support, but true fruit-bearing days come through God and the unity He gifts. A person is not able to build alone unless he steps outside of care and exhorts a lie. Ultimately, he will fail, and all he strived for will perish. When a person invests with the King, he is joined to purity, and life everlasting becomes a way of investing. The knowledge God reigns is a gift no one should ever desire to lose. With this understanding comes the gain of knowing Christ is a caregiver.

Unification with the Most High looks like gold upon the heart. Favor from the hand of God exudes a moral integrity, and light shines forth. Many have forsaken the love of God for money. This is a loss in true understanding. God will always present good. With Satan, money leads as an invitation, but it is not long standing. Life eternal is the map for the truth seeker. If you tarry on the decision as to whether you desire a life of commitment to the Lord, you may find your opportunity washed away. There is no limit to the love of God, but a hardening of the heart happens every time rejection is made. Each opportunity to know the King should be a reason to invite Him in. If you care about your future, make the decision to follow God and be safe in the arms of love. God is available to all mankind, but not all pursue Him.

Set apart your heart for the Lord and gain in the manner all that is good. God will awaken your desire to know Him in a personal way, and this will lead to growth with a directive of unity at its core. God the Father knows your every need. He will support the dream that is made up of goodness and mercy. If you look at where your heart stands, you may learn you claim the King and have already accepted that He is real and just. If this is the case, you are joined to the bride of Christ, and many others are in your court. Lean into the great heart of unity and attend a church where the gospel and the truth of the Word are preached. By doing this action, you will inherit a justified manner, and your goal setting will adhere to the love of God. Your invitation to love others will be recognized, and you will achieve a path forward. God lives within many. Dine on the truth that you are not alone in your discomfort or pain. There are many others with the need for God who, too, long for a friend or member of the body of Christ to instruct them in a personal manner. We are able to support one another by simply being a friend. With love as the goal and purpose of your heart, a building of unity will ensue. God is the one to develop a way ahead, and by His way of being, we learn how to manifest and create in a manner of good intent. It is the desire of man to lead and to present as a unity maker. God has designed man to operate in this form. Whether we wash floors or have gained the title of master over many, our role is to complete the unity of one man to ourselves and to lift up one another in care. Anyone who follows this knowledge is aware there are some who pursue other avenues for their lives. If walking in the way of the Most High goes against your point of view, you are a lost creation. God is the creator, and He made you in His image. The Word of God divulges this as truth. Look at scripture for the portrayal of this unity.

27 So God created man in his own image, in the image of God he created him; male and female he created them. Genesis 2:27 NIV

The call of faith is heard by man if truth is pressed in the spirit and accepted as holy and righteous. If a person bleeds in pain caused by a loss or imprisonment of heartache, be it death or separation of a marriage union, division manifests and causes doubt about the value of oneself. This is why man falls prey to the devil. The work of the enemy of God is to create a falsehood that value is based on another's affection. Understanding God is the true source of man's value can enlighten the heart and feed it truth. When a person believes he is a child of the Most High, value is then recognized, and hope settles in. No one being can lift up another without first understanding the importance of who the Lord is. We can learn the value of God when we invest in reading the Bible. His expression of unity is found in every presentation of the Word. The Book of Psalms carries many to the throne of God as it is uplifting in its guidance. The Book of Psalms contains various authors, but all of them speak the truth. Read it and gain insight that will carry you to God in unity and support.

15 The eyes of the Lord are on the righteous and his ears are attentive to their cry; 16 the face of the Lord is against those who

do evil, to cut off the memory of them from the earth. 17The righteous cry out, and the Lord hears them; he delivers them from all their troubles. 18 The Lord is close to the brokenhearted and saves those who are crushed in spirit. Psalm 34:15-18 NIV

God the Father is a caretaker, and He invests in the people who cleave to Him personally. If you feel unaccompanied, remember the King is always at your side. He grafts to the spirit when it calls His name. This is truth as spoken by many who have encountered the King in their lifestyle. Growing in support of who God is delivers the truth that He is real. If a shoulder seems yielded to the knowledge God is genuine, it is more apt to press in faith and work toward the goal of a companion of the Most High in comparison to standing alone in a marsh of doubt. When you dine on the truth, God supports you. Your bright future is seen and appreciated because you understand God won't forsake you. Man is misguided when it comes to love. The only real unity is by God's hand. He won't lead you into a loss, nor will He make you turn on another. When you pursue Him real understanding of value is built upon. The ladder of hope is made stable when the heart forms a boundary of good intent based on the truth of the Word of God. Each scripture tie is made solid when the heart believes and supports it as God's heart and unity structure. God has a plan for you and me. It is right, and it will incorporate His good name. God does not veer away from a true, glorious union. His goal is always good and purposeful. God is capable of all things righteous. He never sins or brings evil to anyone. If you favor a walk of intent, look at where you place your trust. Do you believe God can work in your favor? Do you support His way of being? If God is your light, you have found favor in Him. God leads with care, and He is righteous in manner. The look of love is God's face alone. People can build relationship unions, but only steadfast support from the Most High will keep you stable and on the path of good manners. Many find love fleeting because they only enjoy the beginning stage of courtship. Love takes work. It takes a manner of good intent.

One must strive to maintain a relationship of honor. Otherwise, enticements of lust will form, and lies will set in. A person who stays faithful does so because he has determined the value of life as a whole.

The commitment to reach a plateau and then stand on its bank shows a unity structure. God is the ultimate way to achieve a union of forthright hope. God brings to man the hope of eternal life. When God calls man to Himself, He gifts the mind with gain. God leads and organizes the unity of Himself to man in the manner of great strength. The King Jesus is always at our side, giving us faith and support so we may lead and instruct just as He does. God operates in the care field as a soldier of great integrity. You can count on God to invest in your person and believe it will always be in a good manner. Never does the Lord give a negative bounty. God does not operate with loss. He is always building and providing a good way forward.

In the region of unity, man gains the knowledge of true faith if he steps toward the goal of love and care. This is what God sees as a gift of fortune. The tower of Babel was torn down as it entertained man to believe he was greater than God. This is a falsehood in the mind of any who seek to serve themselves. Working to build character is always the best decision to pursue. If you hope for more wealth, think about the manner of giving to aid another. God works in the ministry of unity, and He supports the person who shares his gifts with others. It may seem futile, but God will grow an offering, and it will encompass the love of God as it flourishes.

The leverage of a gift is not to be given with strings attached. It represents God's love, and it should carry support, not a loan factor. Caring for others is what brings the Lord close. It is not the only way to drive home the good of God, but it is a way to shower another with care. God invests in all mankind. He freely offers the gift of salvation. In the example of unity here, we gain the truth that God supports us without reservations. He does not expect a payment back. He desires us to love and communicate with Him personally. Our repentance needs to be genuine, and it builds favor with God. Diving into the community of the saved race leads us to the understanding God joins our hearts in care and unity. Why God builds in this manner is a gift we need to accept and adhere to. Our lives are not our own. We are a living sacrifice of the Most High. We aren't expected to offer our health, but we are to give of our spirit. Joy comes forward when we apply our minds to do good. We learn how to lift up others in the manner of faith, and this, in turn, delivers a gain. To man's way of thinking, one should hold tight to material wealth, but this is not the case with light and hope.

How God expresses care is often seen as unwise by a worldly standard. Our light is gifted when we enlist the gain we have one to another. We don't have to spend large amounts to be a representative of the Most High. A simple gesture of offered faith can be recognized as care, and love will be built upon in the manner of trust.

Love is made complete when the heart believes God is who He claims to be. No one can operate on their own. If you have made the decision that God is your team member and He leads you in a righteous way, you have learned good form. The God of the universe supports the world, and He carries all to Him who serve Him and lean into Him as their God. God authors the heart, and in doing so, He divests the mind with good integrity. Anyone offering another way does not know the real I Am, the author of love. God's care supports the mind, so clarity is always known, and hope is present. When a person believes the Father cares for him, he gains an improved understanding he is not alone. God never sways the heart to follow a dark path. When the light of the Most High is visible, a path forward is revealed. God authors all who believe He is who He claims to be. When you look at the way God built up the nation of Israel, you are better equipped to relate to the true manner of Him and how He operates. Throughout the years, God has been enabling the nation of Israel to build a centralized manner of good intent. Israel has a substantial bounty in their homeland, all due to the love and protection of King Jesus. Our God died so we may have eternal life. Israel does not know the truth of their King at this time, but they will one day serve Him alongside all mankind. God is going to return to the earth and stake His name upon the globe. No one will be able to lie and say He doesn't exist, as all will see Him in all His glory. Soon the way we present our heart will be in a face-to-face manner. There will be no doubt or hindrance other than that of free will. Anyone who decides to leave the comfort of the King will find a lifestyle of loss.

God will allow man to choose his own path but know outside of God is death. The cross is the mechanism that enables people to gain entry to the God of all. God, the Father, is our Waymaker. He has provided man with the knowledge of who He is by supplying us with the Word of God called the Bible. It is a simple measure to assume a righteous path because God has provided the footing needed to walk in care, which leads to unity and grace. By the power of God, man can be complete. He can find truth and support with the opportune method of unity in the center of the manifested thought process known as faith. Faith is what determines our unity with God. If you fail in the department of faith, let God build you a fence of protection. Engage in reading and professing that Jesus is Lord, and you will find repentance will ensue, and the gateway to a connection with Him will transpire. God breaks the bond of deception the enemy puts upon your mind. He makes a unity where you reflect and pursue the King with glorious intent, thus tying the heart and setting in motion the love of God to pursue you. When walking in unity, a mind develops with a new outlook, and a manner of good unfolds. God loves all people. He does not discriminate in any form. If you trust in Jesus, you will know Him personally, and a relationship will blossom. The unity of God to you is a gift none can compare to. You won't find a more faithful one to adhere to. The great I Am is all knowing, and He supports your heart always and forever.

The Biography of Robin (Rochel) Arne

Robin is an artist with a flair for the authorship of God to man. She expresses love and concern in her writing. As a child, she loved to read and learn about mankind in the story form, but today she builds up the unity of God to man. Robin designs in clay, and she crafts the heart in doing so. Her work is an expression of unity where her designs speak of scripture and the truth of the Lord in her life. Today Robin works and declares the goodness of God in all she puts forth. Her dream of owning a church is at the forefront of her thoughts. She has faith that God will one day guide her to the home of her desire, but until then, she masters writing and unifying others to the knowledge God always cares about every need. God shoulders Robin, and she understands He alone is her heart's love. All other work and needs come second in her life. God has granted favor to Robin where she hears Him speak the words she puts to paper. She trusts God will provide her the following to be able to continue her craft of writing. Every day is filled with pursuing in faith the Most High. It is counted as joy when typing ensues, and words come forth. God delivers the gain by always providing the funds to publish her work. He has not delayed the process, nor will He. The net worth of Robin is limited, but that alone does not determine her commitment to the detail of transcribing words of faith to paper. Her guidance counselor leads her days, and she enjoys spending time in the Word He provided, called His Bible.

Now is an advancement in time. The day of the rapture looks to be on the horizon, and this spurs the intent of God to embellish to man His heart and call. If you are led to pursue the Most High, today is the time to take action. Gain awaits you if you do, and you will find love has captured your spirit just as it has Robin's. Robin invests in time with God. She is faithful to read her Bible and trusts the words therein. Grace is at the door of her heart. Today she will read and pray for enlightenment to be prepared to reach others in truth. It is the purpose of God to know each person in a personal manner. Robin understands this call and aims to share the Gospel with all who come before her.

Robin (Rochel) Arne

Robin Arne is available for author interviews. For more information
contact us at info@advbooks.com

To purchase additional copies of this book, visit our bookstore at
www.advbookstore.com

Other books by Robin Arne:
God's Manifestation of The Heart   ISBN: 9781597556897
The Hurts Can Be Healed   ISBN: 9781597557108

*A*dvantage
BOOKS

"we bring dreams to life"™
www.advbookstore.com

www.ingramcontent.com/pod-product-compliance
Lightning Source LLC
LaVergne TN
LVHW021525080426
835509LV00018B/2672